Networks Social Studies

Our Community and Beyond

Teacher Edition

THEN & NOW

History Museum

Mc
Graw
Hill
Education

PROGRAM AUTHORS

James A. Banks, Ph.D.
Kerry and Linda Killinger Endowed
    Chair in Diversity Studies and
    Director, Center for Multicultural
    Education
University of Washington
Seattle, Washington

Kevin P. Colleary, Ed.D.
Curriculum and Teaching Department
Graduate School of Education
Fordham University
New York, New York

Linda Greenow, Ph.D.
Associate Professor and Chair
Department of Geography
State University of New York at
    New Paltz
New Paltz, New York

Walter C. Parker, Ph.D.
Professor of Social Studies Education,
    Adjunct Professor of Political
    Science
University of Washington
Seattle, Washington

Emily M. Schell, Ed.D.
Visiting Professor, Teacher Education
San Diego State University
San Diego, California

Dinah Zike
Educational Consultant
Dinah-Might Adventures, L.P.
San Antonio, Texas

CONTRIBUTING AUTHORS

James M. Denham, Ph.D.
Professor of History and Director,
    Lawton M. Chiles, Jr., Center for
    Florida History
Florida Southern College
Lakeland, Florida

M.C. Bob Leonard, Ph.D.
Professor, Hillsborough Community
    College
Director, Florida History Internet
    Center
Ybor City, Florida

Jay McTighe
Educational Author and Consultant
McTighe and Associates Consulting
Columbia, Maryland

Timothy Shanahan, Ph.D.
Professor of Urban Education &
    Director, Center for Literacy
College of Education
University of Illinois at Chicago

ACADEMIC CONSULTANTS

Tom Daccord
Educational Technology Specialist
Co-Director, EdTechTeacher
Boston, Massachusetts

Joe Follman
Service Learning Specialist
Director, Florida Learn & Serve

Cathryn Berger Kaye, M.A.
Service Learning Specialist
Author, *The Complete Guide to
    Service Learning*

Justin Reich
Educational Technology Specialist
Co-Director, EdTechTeacher
Boston, Massachusetts

Send all inquiries to:
McGraw-Hill Education
8787 Orion Place
Columbus, OH 43240

ISBN: 978-0-02-132695-2
MHID: 0-02-132695-9

Printed in the United States of America.

1 2 3 4 5 6 7 8 9 QVS 19 18 17 16 15 14

Common Core State Standards© Copyright 2010. National Governors Association Center
for Best Practices and Council of Chief State School Officers. All rights reserved.

Understanding by Design® is a registered trademark of the
Association for Supervision and Curriculum Development ("ASCD").

TEACHER REVIEWERS

Karen S. Cangemi
Fourth Grade Teacher
Oakhurst Elementary
Largo, Florida

Margaret Claffey
First Grade Teacher
Jerry Thomas Elementary
Jupiter, Florida

Lisa March Folz
Fifth Grade Teacher
Blackburn Elementary
Palmetto, Florida

Amanda Hicks
National Board Certified Teacher,
    Elementary Education
Second Grade Teacher
Hollywood Hills Elementary
Hollywood, Florida

LaKeitha N. Jackson
K-12 Literacy Coach
Fort Pierce Magnet School of
    the Arts
Fort Pierce, Florida

Kimberly B. Kieser
Third Grade Teacher
Woodlawn Elementary
St. Petersburg, Florida

Richard C. Mason
Fourth Grade Teacher
Blackburn Elementary
Palmetto, Florida

Estrella M. Mellon
Fourth Grade Teacher
Stoneman Douglas Elementary
Miami, Florida

Nicki D. Rutkowski, Ed.D.
Kindergarten Teacher
Blackburn Elementary
Palmetto, Florida

Virginia Enriquez Sanchez
National Board Certified Teacher
South Miami K-8 Center
Miami, Florida

Jessica Spiller
First Grade Teacher
Blackburn Elementary
Palmetto, Florida

Table of Contents

UNIT 1 People and Traditions

BIG IDEA 💡 People and events shape history.

UNIT 2 Where We Live

BIG IDEA 💡 Location affects how people live.

Notebook FOLDABLES templates can be found at the end of this book.

Networks Social Studies

tell me

show me ▶

involve me

Start networking!

connected.mcgraw-hill.com

Using Your networks Program

Teacher Planning

Planning pages appear at the beginning of each unit.

• Unit Big Idea

The Big Idea is the major theme that helps students organize and understand information.

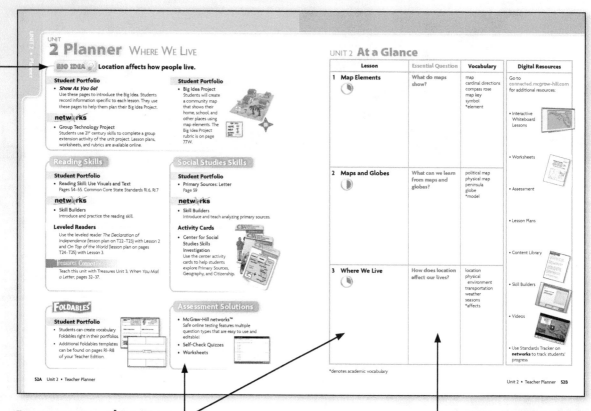

Resources and Lessons at a Glance

Planning made easy.

• Essential Questions

Lesson-specific Essential Questions tie content to the Unit Big Idea.

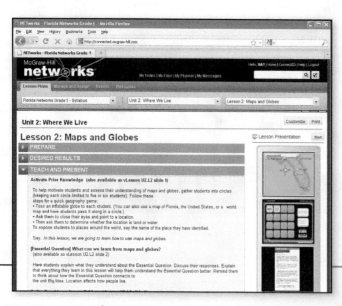

Start netw⊕rking!

Customizable Model Lesson Plans

The online teacher edition features model lesson plans for each lesson. You can customize each lesson plan to fit your time demands and the needs of your students.

Understanding by Design®

Quality instruction develops and deepens student understanding through the use of carefully crafted learning experiences. The **McGraw-Hill networks™** program focuses on teaching for understanding through on-going, inquiry-based instruction and assessment. This program was created through the Understanding by Design® (UbD) curriculum design model. At the core of UbD lies a focus on what is taught and how it is assessed.

In the **networks** program, each unit is centered on a **Big Idea**. The unit Big Idea focuses student learning through the use of prior knowledge and stimulates deeper understanding.

The end of each unit features a **Big Idea Project**. Through this authentic assessment, students demonstrate the understanding gained within the unit. As a final step, students reflect and explain how what they learned affected their understanding of the Big Idea.

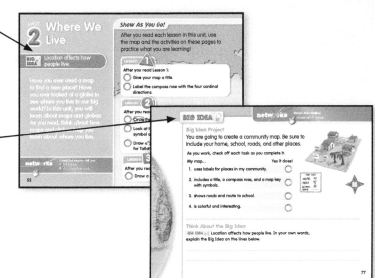

Each lesson focuses on an **Essential Question.** These open-ended questions allow students the opportunity to make connections, view events from different perspectives, and integrate information.

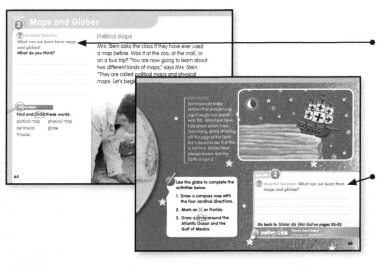

At the end of each lesson, students again respond to the **Essential Question.** This response should reflect a change in student understanding based on their experiences within the lesson.

Contributing Author

Jay McTighe has published articles in a number of leading educational journals and has co-authored ten books, including the best-selling *Understanding By Design* series with Grant Wiggins. Jay also has an extensive background in professional development and is a featured speaker at national, state, and district conferences and workshops. He received his undergraduate degree from The College of William and Mary, earned a Masters degree from The University of Maryland, and completed post-graduate studies at The Johns Hopkins University.

Student Engagement

Each lesson has activities that stimulate learning and interest.

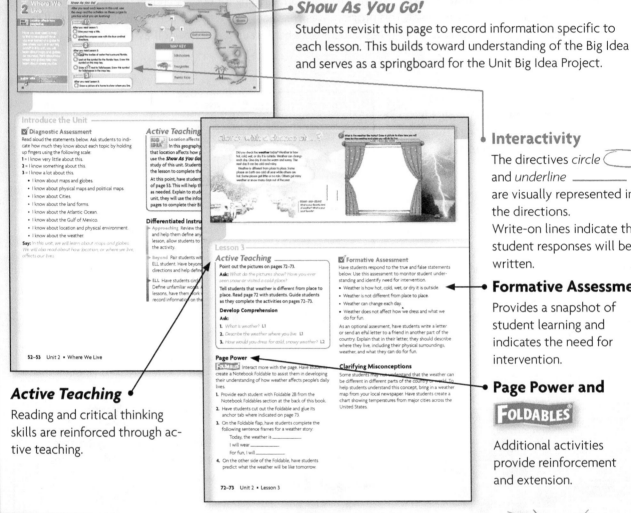

Show As You Go!

Students revisit this page to record information specific to each lesson. This builds toward understanding of the Big Idea and serves as a springboard for the Unit Big Idea Project.

Interactivity

The directives *circle* ⬭ and *underline* ___ are visually represented in the directions.
Write-on lines indicate that student responses will be written.

Formative Assessment

Provides a snapshot of student learning and indicates the need for intervention.

Page Power and FOLDABLES®

Additional activities provide reinforcement and extension.

Active Teaching

Reading and critical thinking skills are reinforced through active teaching.

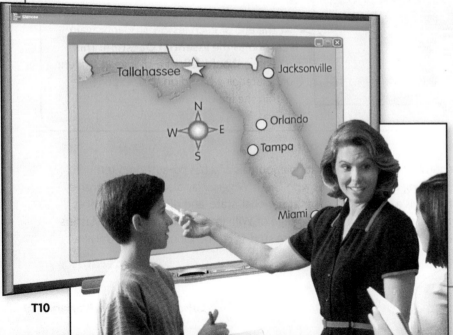

Start networking!

Interactive Whiteboard Lessons

Engage students with these interactive whiteboard activities. vLessons include images, vocabulary, and graphic organizers to enrich and extend Social Studies content. The vLessons and these additional digital resources motivate students and reinforce Social Studies concepts and skills:

- Interactive Maps
- Videos

Reading Integration

Each unit has skills-based instruction that focuses on Common Core State Standards for English Language Arts: Reading Standards for Informational Text.

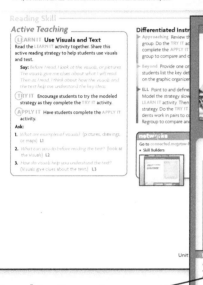

Integrated Reading and Writing Skills

Students learn, try, and apply the skills.

Vocabulary Foldable

After constructing the "stay in the book" Vocabulary Foldable, students complete activities that reinforce word meanings.

Vocabulary Instruction

Content and Academic Vocabulary are taught and reinforced through Foldables, graphic organizers, and games.

Graphic Organizers

Each unit has a different graphic organizer to help students gain a deeper understanding of unit vocabulary and concepts.

Start netw⊙rking!

Interactive Games

Engaging interactive Vocabulary Games help students practice vocabulary and concepts.

The Vocabulary Games and these additional digital resources can be used to introduce and review vocabulary, to reinforce reading skills, and to build comprehension and fluency:

- Vocabulary Flashcards
- Puzzle Maker
- Worksheets
- Graphic Organizers
- Skill Builders
- Audio-Visual Online Student Experience

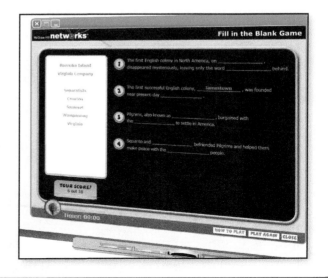

Using Your networks Program

Social Studies Instruction

Skills instruction is spiraled throughout each grade and between grade levels.

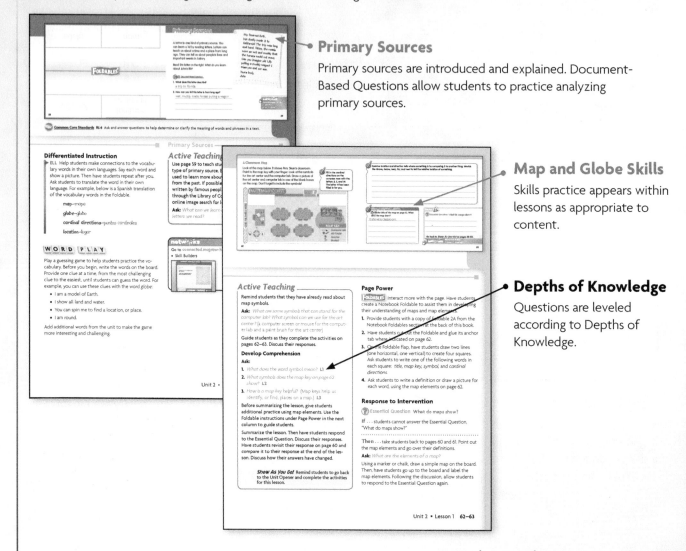

Primary Sources

Primary sources are introduced and explained. Document-Based Questions allow students to practice analyzing primary sources.

Map and Globe Skills

Skills practice appears within lessons as appropriate to content.

Depths of Knowledge

Questions are leveled according to Depths of Knowledge.

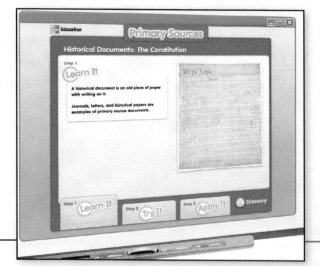

Start networking!

Skill Builders

Interactive learning tools help students use a variety of Social Studies skills. Each tool will allow students to learn, try, and apply each Social Studies skill in an active and engaging way.

• Primary Sources
• Map and Globe Skills
• Chart and Graph Skills

Tell Me • Show Me • Involve Me!

Project and Assessment

Each unit provides a variety of formative and summative assessments, as well as suggested interventions.

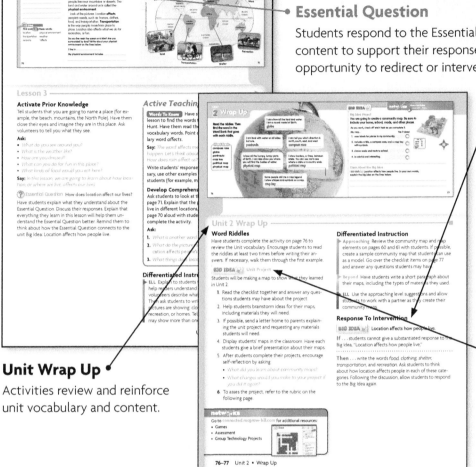

Essential Question

Students respond to the Essential Question using lesson content to support their response. This check provides an opportunity to redirect or intervene for struggling students.

Response To Intervention

Provides intervention options for struggling students.

Unit Wrap Up

Activities review and reinforce unit vocabulary and content.

Big Idea Project

Unit performance tasks require students to synthesize information while creating, presenting, and evaluating a project. Students use a checklist as a guide for working through the project. Each project has a reproducible project rubric for scoring.

Start networking!

Self-Check Quizzes

Self-Check Quizzes gauge students' level of understanding before, during, or after studying a lesson. The Self-Check Quizzes and these additional resources are available for formative, summative, or project-based assessment.

- McGraw-Hill networks™ Assessment
- Group Technology Project

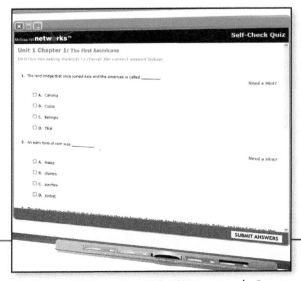

Differentiated Instruction

Differentiated instruction activities meet the diverse needs of every student.

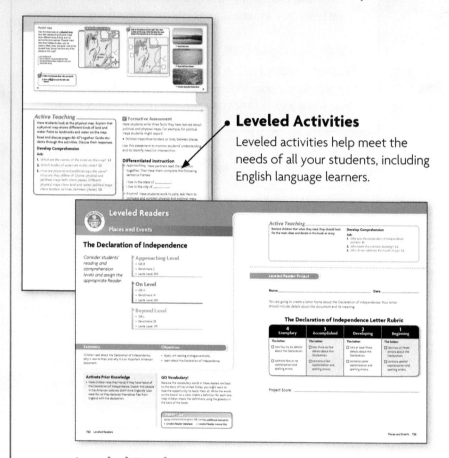

Leveled Activities

Leveled activities help meet the needs of all your students, including English language learners.

Center Card Activity Kit

Students investigate Primary Sources, Geography, and Citizenship.

Leveled Readers

One topic presented at three different reading levels provides an opportunity for your whole class to participate in a discussion about the topic.

- ### Content Library

  There's more to learn in the Content Library! A bank of short articles provides background information about topics covered in each unit. Use the Content Library to enrich or extend student knowledge beyond information presented in the text.

- ### Access Points

  Access Points activities for standards are available in your customizable model lesson plans. Here you will find independent, supported, and participatory activities to meet the needs of your students.

- ### Character Education

  Develop the character of your students with our Character Education curriculum. Students have the opportunity to explain, explore, experience, and exhibit a variety of character traits through cooperative activities and self-reflection.

- ### Service Learning

  Make Service Learning simple and easy with step-by-step guidance to enrich the learning experience of your students. Use hands-on, real world projects to develop skills, behaviors, and habits of good citizenship.

Levels of Cognitive Complexity

Questions throughout your Teacher Edition are labeled L1 (Level 1),
L2 (Level 2), or L3 (Level 3) depending upon their level of complexity.

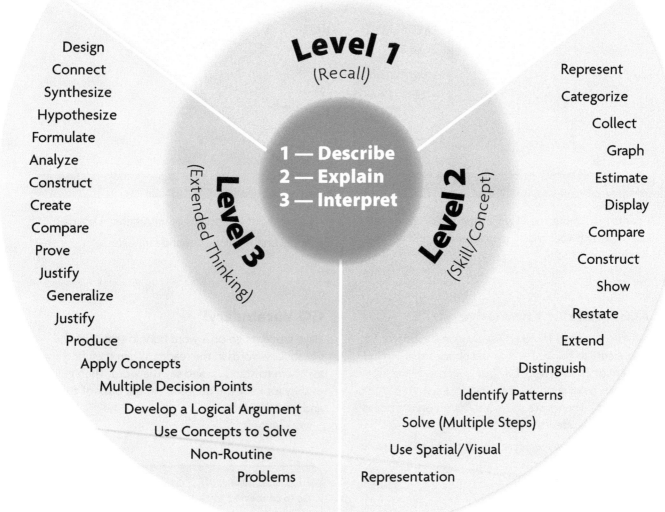

Draw

Identify   Recognize   List

Retrieve   Procedure   Compute   Define

Match   Recite   State   Measure

Recall   Tell   Name

                                    Solve (1 Step)

Level 1
(Recall)

Design
Connect
Synthesize
Hypothesize
Formulate
Analyze
Construct
Create
Compare
Prove
Justify
Generalize
Justify
Produce
Apply Concepts
Multiple Decision Points
Develop a Logical Argument
Use Concepts to Solve
Non-Routine
Problems

Level 3
(Extended Thinking)

1 — Describe
2 — Explain
3 — Interpret

Level 2
(Skill/Concept)

Represent
Categorize
Collect
Graph
Estimate
Display
Compare
Construct
Show
Restate
Extend
Distinguish
Identify Patterns
Solve (Multiple Steps)
Use Spatial/Visual
Representation

The First Thanksgiving

Consider students' reading and comprehension levels and assign the appropriate Reader.

▶ **Approaching Level**
- GR: C
- Benchmark: 4
- Lexile Level: 190

▶ **On Level**
- GR: I
- Benchmark: 16
- Lexile Level: 510

▶ **Beyond Level**
- GR: L
- Benchmark: 24
- Lexile Level: 580

Summary

Students read about the Pilgrims' first Thanksgiving feast, including why it took place, who attended, and why we still celebrate it today.

Objectives

- Learn about the origins of an American holiday.
- Apply unit reading skills and strategies.

Activate Prior Knowledge

- Write the term *Thanksgiving Day* on the board. Ask students to think of words and phrases that remind them of Thanksgiving Day (for example, giving thanks, helping others, celebration, feast, turkey, and so forth). Then write the word *Pilgrim* on the board and have students repeat the activity.
- Explain that they will read about the Pilgrims' first Thanksgiving.

GO Vocabulary!

Have students go on a word hunt in search of the vocabulary words in the reader. When they find a word, ask them to stand up and say the word. Then guide them as they look for the definition in the back of the glossary and read the definition.

networks

Go to connected.mcgraw-hill.com for additional resources:
- Leveled Reader Database
- Leveled Reader Answer Key

Active Teaching

As students read, encourage them to think about the events in the story. Provide students with copies of a summarizing chart or graphic organizer. Ask them to summarize the story about the Pilgrims' first Thanksgiving.

Develop Comprehension

Ask:

1. *How did the Native Americans help the Pilgrims?* **L1**

2. **Compare and Contrast** *How are the Pilgrims and the Native Americans the same? How are they different?* (Native Americans: first people to settle the area; Pilgrims: people from England who came to America; Same: live in America; need food, clothes, and shelter to survive) **L3**

3. **Compare and Contrast** *How is Thanksgiving Day today the same or different from the Pilgrims' first Thanksgiving?* **L3**

Leveled Reader Project

Name _____ Date _____

Imagine that you are a Pilgrim or a Native American who helped the Pilgrims survive their first winter. You are going to act out the events you read about in *The First Thanksgiving*.

Skit Rubric

4 Exemplary	3 Accomplished	2 Developing	1 Beginning
The skit:	**The skit:**	**The skit:**	**The skit:**
☐ accurately portrays events and characters.	☐ somewhat accurately portrays events and characters.	☐ attempts to portray events and characters.	☐ lacks understanding of events and characters.
☐ uses many words and phrases appropriate to the events.	☐ uses words and phrases appropriate to the events.	☐ attempts to use words and phrases appropriate to the events.	☐ may use some words and phrases appropriate to the events.
☐ shows artistic interpretation.	☐ shows overall artistic interpretation.	☐ attempts to show artistic interpretation	☐ does not show artistic interpretation.

Project Score: _____

Daniel Inouye

Consider students' reading and comprehension levels and assign the appropriate Reader.

▶ Approaching Level
- GR: C
- Benchmark: 3
- Lexile Level: 210

▶ On Level
- GR: G
- Benchmark: 12
- Lexile Level: 290

▶ Beyond Level
- GR: K
- Benchmark: 20
- Lexile Level: 400

Summary

Students read about the life of Daniel Inouye, including his childhood, his heroic acts during Pearl Harbor and World War II, and how he became a senator after the war.

Objectives

- Learn about Daniel Inouye's contributions as a war veteran and leader.
- Apply reading strategies and skills.

Activate Prior Knowledge

- Ask students to list character traits associated with a leader. Encourage them to think about how leaders display honesty and responsibility and lead by example.
- Remind students that they have already read about leaders who showed honesty and responsibility. Explain that they will now read about another American leader.

GO Vocabulary!

Organize students into their leveled reading groups. Provide index cards for each group. Ask students to write a vocabulary word on one side of each card and the definition on the other side. Then, have one student read the definition while the others guess the word.

networks

Go to connected.mcgraw-hill.com for additional resources:
- Leveled Reader Database
- Leveled Reader Answer Key

Active Teaching

Display a world map or a globe. Point out Hawaii and Japan on the map or globe. Tell students that Hawaii is one of the 50 states in the United States. Explain that it became a state in 1960. Tell students that many people of Japanese descent live in Hawaii because Hawaii and Japan aren't very far from each other. Now ask if anyone has heard about Pearl Harbor. Tell students that Pearl Harbor is in Hawaii. Explain that an incident in Pearl Harbor led to America's involvement in World War II.

Develop Comprehension

Ask:

1. *What happened in Pearl Harbor in 1941?* (Pearl Harbor was bombed.) **L1**
2. **Main Idea and Details** *What was Daniel's childhood like?* (lived in Hawaii; grew up poor; played baseball; played with pigeons) **L2**
3. **Main Idea and Details** *What important things did Daniel do?* (helped people who were hurt in Pearl Harbor; joined the army; became a hero; went to law school; became a senator) **L2**

Leveled Reader Project

Name _____ Date _____

Write a paragraph that tells about a hero you know or have read about. After you have written your paragraph, draw a picture of your hero.

Hero Essay Rubric

4 Exemplary	3 Accomplished	2 Developing	1 Beginning
The essay:	**The essay:**	**The essay:**	**The essay:**
☐ includes a main idea and at least three or four details.	☐ includes a main idea and at least two or three details.	☐ includes a main idea and at least one or two details.	☐ does not include a main idea or details.
☐ contains few or no errors in capitalization and spelling.	☐ contains a few errors in capitalization and spelling.	☐ contains some capitalization and spelling errors.	☐ contains several capitalization and spelling errors.
☐ includes a drawing that clearly shows someone who is a hero.	☐ includes a drawing that shows someone who is a hero.	☐ includes a drawing that somewhat shows a picture of a hero.	☐ does not include a drawing or the drawing is not clear.

Project Score: _____

Coretta Scott King

Consider students' reading and comprehension levels and assign the appropriate Reader.

▶ Approaching Level
- GR: B
- Benchmark: 2
- Lexile Level: 170

▶ On Level
- GR: F
- Benchmark: 10
- Lexile Level: 230

▶ Beyond Level
- GR: L
- Benchmark: 24
- Lexile Level: 690

Summary

Children read about the life of Coretta Scott King, including her childhood, her work with her husband Martin Luther King, Jr., and how she continued civil rights work throughout her life.

Objectives

- Apply unit reading strategies and skills.
- Learn about the importance of civil rights.

Activate Prior Knowledge

- Ask children if they have ever heard of Martin Luther King, Jr. Invite them to tell you what they know about him. Explain that Coretta Scott King was Dr. King's wife and partner in the crusade for civil rights.

GO Vocabulary!

On the board, write some of the vocabulary words from the reader (*civil rights, fair, freedom*). Discuss the meanings of each word. Have children cut out pictures from a magazine that illustrate fairness and freedom. Tell them that civil rights helps to make sure everyone has the same freedoms and are treated fairly.

networks

Go to connected.mcgraw-hill.com for additional resources:
- Leveled Reader Database
- Leveled Reader Answer Key

Active Teaching

Remind children that when they compare and contrast things, they learn about their differences and their similarities. Write the following questions on the board:

Develop Comprehension

Ask:

1. *Were all people treated fairly before the civil rights movement?* **L1**
2. *How has life changed since then?* **L2**
3. *How are things the same?* **L2**

Leveled Reader Project

Name _____ **Date** _____

Create a poster that tells others about the life of Coretta Scott King. The posters could involve her early life in school or her life as a civil rights leader.

Coretta Scott King Poster Rubric

4 Exemplary	3 Accomplished	2 Developing	1 Beginning
The poster:	**The poster:**	**The poster:**	**The poster:**
☐ clearly shows about Coretta Scott King's life.	☐ shows some about Coretta Scott King's life.	☐ tries to show about Coretta Scott King's life.	☐ does not show about Coretta Scott King's life.
☐ is creative, colorful, and interesting.	☐ is somewhat creative, colorful, and interesting.	☐ tries to show creativity, color, and visual interest.	☐ lacks creativity and is not visually interesting.
☐ contains few or no errors in capitalization and spelling.	☐ contains a few capitalization and spelling errors.	☐ contains some capitalization and spelling errors.	☐ contains several capitalization and spelling errors.

Project Score: _____

The Declaration of Independence

Consider students' reading and comprehension levels and assign the appropriate Reader.

▶ Approaching Level
- GR: B
- Benchmark: 2
- Lexile Level: 300

▶ On Level
- GR: H
- Benchmark: 14
- Lexile Level: 340

▶ Beyond Level
- GR: L
- Benchmark: 24
- Lexile Level: 510

Summary

Children read about the Declaration of Independence, why it was written, and why it is an important American document.

Objectives

- Apply unit reading strategies and skills.
- Learn about the Declaration of Independence.

Activate Prior Knowledge
- Have children raise their hands if they have heard of the Declaration of Independence. Explain that people in the American colonies didn't think England's rules were fair, so they declared themselves free from England with the declaration.

GO Vocabulary!

Because the vocabulary words in these readers are basic to the story of the United States, you might want to take the opportunity to teach them all. Write the words on the board. As a class, create a definition for each one. Help children check the definitions using the glossary in the back of the book.

networks
Go to connected.mcgraw-hill.com for additional resources:
- Leveled Reader Database
- Leveled Reader Answer Key

Active Teaching

Remind children that when they read, they should look for the main ideas and details in the book or story.

Develop Comprehension

Ask:

1. *Why was the Declaration of Independence written?* **L1**
2. *What were the colonists declaring?* **L2**
3. *Why do we celebrate the Fourth of July?* **L1**

Leveled Reader Project

Name _____ Date _____

You are going to create a letter home about the Declaration of Independence. Your letter should include details about the document and its meaning.

The Declaration of Independence Letter Rubric

4 Exemplary	3 Accomplished	2 Developing	1 Beginning
The letter:	**The letter:**	**The letter:**	**The letter:**
☐ lists four to six details about the Declaration.	☐ lists three to five details about the Declaration.	☐ lists at least three details about the Declaration.	☐ lists two or fewer details about the Declaration.
☐ contains few or no capitalization and spelling errors.	☐ contains a few capitalization and spelling errors.	☐ contains some capitalization and spelling errors.	☐ contains several capitalization and spelling errors.

Project Score: _____

On Top of the World

Consider students' reading and comprehension levels and assign the appropriate Reader.

▶ Approaching Level
- GR: B
- Benchmark: 2
- Lexile Level: 110

▶ On Level
- GR: F
- Benchmark: 10
- Lexile Level: 280

▶ Beyond Level
- GR: K
- Benchmark: 20
- Lexile Level: 460

Summary

Students read about Barrow, Alaska. Barrow is the northernmost city in the United States. It is cold there much of the year. The sun shines all summer long, and it is dark all winter.

Objectives

- Learn about the geography of Barrow, Alaska, and its people.
- Apply reading strategies and skills.

Activate Prior Knowledge

- Have students do a picture walk of the leveled reader. Ask them to predict what they will read about.
- Lead the class in a discussion about Alaska. **Ask:** *What do you know about Alaska?* Explain to students that they will be reading about a place called Barrow, Alaska.

GO Vocabulary!

Preview the vocabulary words in the readers by asking students to guess what they think the words mean.

Northern Lights   snowmobile   celebrate

parkas   festival   temperatures

Write students' responses on the board. Then have volunteers read the definitions in the glossary.

networks

Go to **connected.mcgraw-hill.com** for additional resources:
- Leveled Reader Database
- Leveled Reader Answer Key

Active Teaching

Display a map of the United States or use a globe to point out the location of Alaska. Explain that Barrow, Alaska, is the northernmost city in the United States. Remind students that they have learned how location affects people's homes, food, transportation, and recreation.

Develop Comprehension

Ask:

1. *How do people get around in Barrow, Alaska?* (dog-sleds, snowmobiles, airplanes) **L1**
2. **Classify** *What is life like in Barrow?* (fish and hunt for food, dark in winter, all-day sun in summer) **L2**
3. **Compare and Contrast** *How is life in Barrow the same or different from your life?* **L3**

Leveled Reader Project

Name _____ Date _____

Your job is to create a mobile to show what you have learned about Barrow, Alaska. Go back through the reader *On Top of the World* and write down ideas for homes, food, transportation, and clothes. Draw and label four pictures that show how people live in Barrow. When you are finished, attach the pictures to a clothes hanger.

Mobile Rubric

4 Exemplary	3 Accomplished	2 Developing	1 Beginning
The mobile: ☐ shows a picture for homes, food, clothes and transportation in Barrow, Alaska. ☐ contains labels for each picture with no capitalization and spelling errors.	**The mobile:** ☐ shows two or three pictures about Barrow, Alaska. ☐ contains labels for each picture with few capitalization and spelling errors.	**The mobile:** ☐ may show one or two pictures about Barrow, Alaska. ☐ contains few labels for each picture with some capitalization and spelling errors.	**The mobile:** ☐ does not show any pictures about Barrow, Alaska. ☐ may contain labels for each picture with serious capitalization and spelling errors.

Project Score: _____

Leveled Readers

Jobs at School

Consider students' reading and comprehension levels and assign the appropriate Reader.

▶ Approaching Level
- GR: C
- Benchmark: 3
- Lexile Level: 230

▶ On Level
- GR: H
- Benchmark: 14
- Lexile Level: 340

▶ Beyond Level
- GR: K
- Benchmark: 20
- Lexile Level: 540

Summary

Students read about school workers and the services they provide.

Objectives

- Learn about different service jobs in school.
- Apply reading strategies and skills.

Activate Prior Knowledge

- Ask students to list the school jobs they know and the roles and responsibilities for each job.
- If possible, ask the principal, librarian, nurse, or another school worker to give a brief speech about their job, including their responsibilities.

GO Vocabulary!

Provide a scrap sheet of paper for each student. Give clues for each vocabulary word and ask students to guess the word for each clue. Go over the words and the definitions with students.

networks

Go to connected.mcgraw-hill.com for additional resources:
- Leveled Reader Database
- Leveled Reader Answer Key

Active Teaching

Explain to students that the reader *Jobs at School* shows cause-and-effect relationships. As students read the reader, have them fill out a cause-and-effect graphic organizer.

Develop Comprehension

Ask:

1. *What are the names of some of the jobs of school workers?* (teachers, principals, nurses, librarians, cooks, custodians) **L1**

2. **Cause and Effect** *How do teachers help students?* (Cause: Teachers use books, Internet, and other tools to teach. Effect: Students learn to read and write. They also learn math.) **L3**

3. **Cause and Effect** *What would happen if schools did not have principals?* **L3**

Leveled Reader Project

Name _____ Date _____

You are going to create your own book about jobs in school. You can include any of the following jobs: teacher, principal, librarian, nurse, media specialist, aide, custodian, or cook.

School Jobs Rubric

4 Exemplary	3 Accomplished	2 Developing	1 Beginning
The book:	**The book:**	**The book:**	**The book:**
☐ includes correct information from the book.	☐ includes some information from the book.	☐ tries to include information from the book.	☐ does not include information from the book.
☐ is easy to read and is interesting.	☐ is mostly easy to read and is interesting.	☐ is somewhat easy to read and interesting.	☐ is not easy to read and lacks visual appeal.
☐ contains few or no errors in capitalization and spelling.	☐ contains a few errors in capitalization and spelling.	☐ contains some errors in capitalization and spelling.	☐ contains several errors in capitalization and spelling.

Project Score: _____

The Apple Man:
The Story of John Chapman

Consider students' reading and comprehension levels and assign the appropriate Reader.

▶ Approaching Level
- GR: B
- Benchmark: 2
- Lexile Level: 250

▶ On Level
- GR: H
- Benchmark: 14
- Lexile Level: 280

▶ Beyond Level
- GR: I
- Benchmark: 16
- Lexile Level: 430

Summary

Students read about the life of John Chapman, more commonly known as Johnny Appleseed. They will read about his love of nature and trees and how he grew and sold apple trees.

Objectives

- Learn about John Chapman as a producer and seller of apples.
- Apply reading skills and strategies.

Activate Prior Knowledge

- Give students a scrap sheet of paper or an index card. Explain that you are going to read clues about a good that is grown. Say each clue at least twice: *I grow on trees. I come in many sizes. I am often red. I am crunchy.* Encourage students to listen to all the clues before writing their answer. Continue until all students have guessed the correct answer.
- Tell students that apples are goods grown by producers. Explain that they will read about John Chapman, better known as Johnny Appleseed.

GO Vocabulary!

Discuss the meaning of these words:

traded   canoe   orchard

pioneers

After discussing the meanings, organize the class into their reading level groups. Have each group draw a picture illustrating the words. Have groups share their pictures.

networks

Go to connected.mcgraw-hill.com for additional resources:
- Leveled Reader Database
- Leveled Reader Answer Key

Active Teaching

As students read, ask them to think about the ways that John Chapman helped others. Provide students with a main idea graphic organizer. Have them write details that show how John Chapman helped people.

Develop Comprehension

Ask:

1. *What good and service did John Chapman provide?* (service: planted apple seeds; good: apples) **L1**

2. **Main Idea and Details** *Who was John Chapman?* (John Chapman lived a long time ago. He loved nature. He left home and traveled to many states. He planted apple seeds.) **L3**

3. **Main Idea and Details** *How did John Chapman help our country?* (He planted many apple seeds. He sold appple trees to pioneers to plant out west. We have apple trees in many states because of him.) **L3**

Leveled Reader Project

Name _____ **Date** _____

Use the reader *The Apple Man: The Story of John Chapman* to create a picture time line of John Chapman's life. Draw pictures to show events in John's life on your time line. Write a sentence for each event.

Time Line Rubric

4 Exemplary	3 Accomplished	2 Developing	1 Beginning
The time line:	**The time line:**	**The time line:**	**The time line:**
☐ Includes four to five events and pictures in the order that they happened.	☐ includes at least four events and pictures in the order that they happened.	☐ includes two to three events and pictures in the order that they happened.	☐ may include some events and pictures in the order that they happened.
☐ includes a sentence describing each event.	☐ includes a sentence describing each event.	☐ tries to include a sentence describing each event.	☐ may include a sentence describing each event.
☐ contains few or no capitalization and spelling errors.	☐ contains a few capitalization and spelling errors.	☐ contains some capitalization and spelling errors.	☐ contains several capitalization and spelling errors.

Project Score: _____

Jane Addams and the House That Helped

Consider students' reading and comprehension levels and assign the appropriate Reader.

▶ Approaching Level
- GR: C
- Benchmark: 3
- Lexile Level: 160

▶ On Level
- GR: G
- Benchmark: 12
- Lexile Level: 380

▶ Beyond Level
- GR: L
- Benchmark: 24
- Lexile Level: 550

Summary

Students will read about the life and contributions of Jane Addams, including her childhood and her work at Hull House, where she helped immigrants learn English, get jobs, and have a better way of life.

Objectives

- Learn about Jane Addams' contributions to her community.
- Apply reading skills and strategies.

Activate Prior Knowledge

- Ask students to imagine they have moved to a new country. Ask: *What sorts of things do you think you would need help with?*

GO Vocabulary!

Use a word web and have students list other words associated with these vocabulary words:

immigrant   neighborhood   day care

Then have students write a sentence about each vocabulary word.

networks

Go to connected.mcgraw-hill.com for additional resources:
- Leveled Reader Database
- Leveled Reader Answer Key

Active Teaching

Have students use the headings and pictures in the book to predict how Jane Addams helped people in her neighborhood. Tell students that Hull House is located in Chicago. Locate Chicago, Illinois, on a map.

Develop Comprehension

Ask:

1. *What was Hull House?* (Hull House was a place where people could come and learn English and get help getting jobs.) **L1**

2. **Cause and Effect** *What did Jane Addams do to help people?* (Jane opened Hull House to help others. Many people came to Hull House to learn English and to get jobs.) **L2**

3. *What are some ways to help others?* **L2**

Leveled Reader Project

Name _____ Date _____

As a class, think of a service project for your school, such as a school supplies drive or a gently-used clothing drive. Create a poster that tells the school about the service project, including the date or dates. Ask for permission to display the posters in the school. You may wish to ask parents and teachers to help carry out the service project.

Service Project Poster Rubric

4 Exemplary	3 Accomplished	2 Developing	1 Beginning
The poster:	**The poster:**	**The poster:**	**The poster:**
☐ clearly explains the service project.	☐ clearly explains the service project.	☐ tries to explain the service project.	☐ has serious problems explaining the service project.
☐ is colorful, creative, and interesting.	☐ is mostly colorful, creative, and interesting.	☐ is somewhat colorful, creative, and interesting.	☐ lacks color and creativity and is not interesting.
☐ contains few or no capitalization and spelling errors.	☐ contains a few capitalization and spelling errors.	☐ contains some capitalization and spelling errors.	☐ contains several capitalization and spelling errors.

Project Score: _____

Common Core State Standards

English Language Arts & Literacy in History/Social Studies, Science, and Technical Subjects

Reading Standards for Informational Text, Grade 1

Standards		Student Pages	Teacher Pages
Key Ideas and Details			
1.	Ask and answer questions about key details in a text.	136	136–137
2.	Identify the main topic and retell the key details of a text.	80–81, 97	80–81
3.	Describe the connection between two individuals, events, ideas, or pieces of information in a text.	28, 36	28–29, 36–37, 92–93, 98–99
Craft and Structure			
4.	Ask and answer questions to help determine or clarify the meaning of words and phrases in a text.	6–8, 43, 47, 56–58, 82–84, 110–111, 112, 116	46–47, 56–57, 58–59, 82–83, 110–111, 116–117
5.	Know and use various text features (e.g., headings, tables of contents, glossaries, electronic menus, icons) to locate key facts or information in a text.	33	32–33, 42–43
6.	Distinguish between information provided by pictures or other illustrations and information provided by the words in a text.	54–55, 68	54–55
Integration of Knowledge and Ideas			
7.	Use the illustrations and details in a text to describe its key ideas.	54–55, 68	54–55
8.	Identify the reasons an author gives to support points in a text.	108–109, 134, 137	108–109
9.	Identify basic similarities in and differences between two texts on the same topic (e.g., in illustrations, descriptions, or procedures).	4–5, 16, 19	16–17, 18–19, 44–45
Range of Reading and Level of Text Complexity			
10.	With prompting and support, read informational texts appropriately complex for grade 1.	*	*

* The McGraw-Hill networks™ program is designed to provide ample opportunity to practice the reading and comprehension of informational texts for history/social studies for grade 1. The use of this book will help students master this standard.

Teacher Notes

UNIT
1 Planner PEOPLE AND TRADITIONS

 **BIG IDEA** **People and events shape history.**

Student Portfolio

- **Show As You Go!**
  Use these pages to introduce the Big Idea. Students record information specific to each lesson. They use these pages to help them plan their Big Idea Project.

netw⊗rks

- **Group Technology Project**
  Students use 21ˢᵗ century skills to complete a group extension activity of the unit project. Lesson plans, worksheets, and rubrics are available online.

Student Portfolio

- **Big Idea Project**
  Students will make a poster about life in the past that will be placed in a classroom museum. The Big Idea Project rubric is on page 51W.

🏠 HOME LIFE

This is life long ago. It is different from life today. Long ago, there was a milkman who would leave milk at your door. Some things are still the same. We still watch t.v. and cook our meals.

Reading Skills

Student Portfolio

- **Reading Skill: Finding Similarities and Differences**
  Pages 4–5. Common Core State Standards RI.9

netw⊗rks

- **Skill Builders**
  Introduce and practice the reading skill.

Leveled Readers

Use the leveled reader *The First Thanksgiving* (lesson plan on pages T16–T17) with Lesson 2; *Daniel Inouye* (lesson plan on pages T18–T19) with Lesson 3; *Coretta Scott King* (lesson plan on T20–T21) with Lesson 3.

Treasures Connection

Teach this unit with Treasures Unit 1, *How You Grew*, pages 70–77 and Unit 3, *Gram and Me*, pages 128–147.

Social Studies Skills

Student Portfolio

- **Primary Sources: Artifacts**
  Page 9

netw⊗rks

- **Skill Builders**
  Introduce and teach analyzing primary sources.

Activity Cards

- **Center for Social Studies Skills Investigation**
  Use the center activity cards to help students explore Primary Sources, Geography, and Citizenship.

FOLDABLES®

Student Portfolio

- Students can create vocabulary Foldables right in their portfolios.
- Additional Foldables templates can be found on pages R1–R8 of your Teacher Edition.

Assessment Solutions

- **McGraw-Hill networks™**
  Safe online testing features multiple question types that are easy to use and editable!
- **Self-Check Quizzes**
- **Worksheets**

UNIT 1 At a Glance

	Lesson	Essential Question	Vocabulary	Digital Resources
1	Change Over Time	How has life changed over time?	history time line community technology *fact	Go to connected.mcgraw-hill.com for additional resources: • Interactive Whiteboard Lessons
2	Special Holidays	Why do we celebrate people and events?	holiday slavery culture *celebration	• Worksheets • Assessment
3	American Heroes	How do people show character?	character *honesty *courage *responsibility	• Lesson Plans • Content Library • Skill Builders
4	Sharing Stories	Why do we read stories?	tall tale fable nonfiction fiction *exaggerate	• Videos • Use Standards Tracker on **networks** to track students' progress.

*denotes academic vocabulary

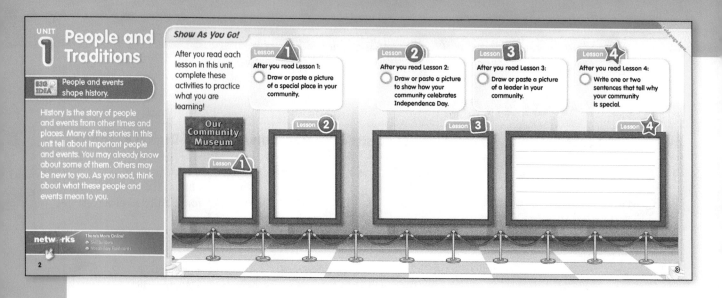

People and events shape history.

History is the story of people and events from other times and places. Many of the stories in this unit tell about important people and events. You may already know about some of them. Others may be new to you. As you read, think about what these people and events mean to you.

net**w**rks There's More Online!
• Skill Builders
• Vocabulary Flashcards

2

Show As You Go!

After you read each lesson in this unit, complete these activities to practice what you are learning!

Lesson 1
After you read Lesson 1:
○ Draw or paste a picture of a special place in your community.

Lesson 2
After you read Lesson 2:
○ Draw or paste a picture to show how your community celebrates Independence Day.

Lesson 3
After you read Lesson 3:
○ Draw or paste a picture of a leader in your community.

Lesson 4
After you read Lesson 4:
○ Write one or two sentences that tell why your community is special.

Our Community Museum

Lesson 1

Lesson 2

Lesson 3

Lesson 4

3

Introduce the Unit

✔ Diagnostic Assessment

Put a variety of objects in a bag. Examples might be a a book, a small bag of animal food, a pencil, etc. Now have a student come up and choose an object out of the bag. When they hold up that object, ask them what this object might tell them about the person who owns it. For example, if the student holds up the bag of animal food, they would say the person has an animal. They might even mention the type of animal it is if it's listed on the bag. After all of the objects have been examined by the class, ask them what objects, people, or events might mean something to them. Explain to the students that objects can tell us a lot about history.

Active Teaching

BIG IDEA **People and events shape history.**
In this unit about people and traditions, students will learn how people and events shape history. As they read each lesson, students will use information from the lesson to complete these pages.

At this point, have students fold back the corner of this page. This will help them flip back to these pages as needed. Explain to students that at the end of the unit, they will use the information collected on these pages to complete their Unit Project.

Differentiated Instruction

▶ **Approaching** Read the checklist items for students. Provide assistance to help students complete the checklist items after each lesson.

▶ **Beyond** Have students write captions for the pictures using vocabulary words from each lesson.

▶ **ELL** Read the checklist items with students. Say the key words in the checklist and have students repeat them after you. Paraphrase the directions, if necessary.

Reading Skill

Common Core Standards
RI.9. Identify basic similarities and differences between two texts on the same topic.

Finding Similarities and Differences

When you read, think about how things are similar or different. Things that are similar are the same in some ways. Things that are different are not the same.

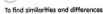

Learn It

To find similarities and differences:
1. Read the stories and look at the pictures.
2. Ask yourself how they are the same.
3. Ask how they are different.

Hi! My name is Sarah. I have chores at home. Before I go to school, I milk the cows and feed the chickens.

Hi! My name is Ava. I have chores, too! On Saturdays, I clean my room and help take out the trash.

Same

Different

Try It

Write the similarities and differences from the story on page 4 in the chart below. Write what is different between Sarah and Ava in the outer circles. Write what is the same in the middle.

Same
Sarah Ava

milk cows and feed chickens

have chores

clean my room and take out the trash

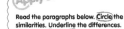

Apply It

Read the paragraphs below. Circle the similarities. Underline the differences.

Long ago, children went to school in one-room schoolhouses. Children of all ages learned together.

Today, most children go to school in big buildings. Most of the time, each class has its own room.

4

5

Common Core Standards RI.9: Identify basic similarities and differences between two texts on the same topic (e.g. in illustrations, descriptions, and procedures).

Reading Skill

Active Teaching

◯ LEARN IT

Finding Similarities and Differences

Read the first paragraph together. Share this active reading strategy for finding similarities and differences:

Say: *As I read, I ask myself, "What things are the same in this story?" Answering this question helps me to find the similarities of the story. Once I know the similarities of the story, I ask "What things are different in this story?" Answering this question helps me to find the differences of the story.*

◯ TRY IT
Encourage students to try the modeled strategy as they complete the TRY IT activity.

◯ APPLY IT
After students have completed the APPLY IT activity,

Ask:

1. *What question should you ask yourself to help you find similarities?* (What is the same?) **L1**

2. *How can pictures help you find similarities and differences?* (compare what is the same and what is different) **L2**

3. *Why is it important to find similarities and differences in a story?* **L3**

Differentiated Instruction

▶ **Approaching** Review the LEARN IT activity as a small group. Do the TRY IT activity together. Have students complete the APPLY IT activity independently. Regroup to compare and correct.

▶ **Beyond** Have students write a short paragraph that includes a similarity and a difference between two characters. Have them exchange paragraphs with a partner. Each student should identify the similarities and differences of their partner's paragraph.

▶ **ELL** Have students discuss the images and predict what the passages might be about. Explain *similarities*. Read the passage one sentence at a time and have students identify similarities. List students' responses. Read the list you have developed. Now do the same with *differences*. Have students discuss how identifying similarities and differences helps them to understand the passage.

networks

Go to **connected.mcgraw-hill.com** for additional resources:
- Skill Builders
- Graphic Organizers

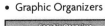

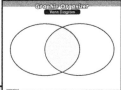

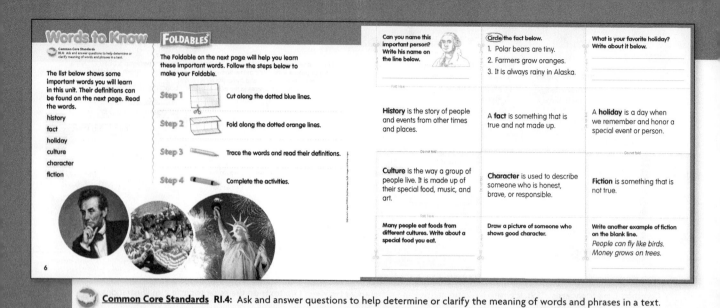

Words to Know FOLDABLES

Common Core Standards
RI.4: Ask and answer questions to help determine or clarify meaning of words and phrases in a text.

The list below shows some important words you will learn in this unit. Their definitions can be found on the next page. Read the words.

history
fact
holiday
culture
character
fiction

The Foldable on the next page will help you learn these important words. Follow the steps below to make your Foldable.

Step 1 — Cut along the dotted blue lines.

Step 2 — Fold along the dotted orange lines.

Step 3 — Trace the words and read their definitions.

Step 4 — Complete the activities.

Can you name this important person? Write his name on the line below.

_____

Circle the fact below.
1. Polar bears are tiny.
2. Farmers grow oranges.
3. It is always rainy in Alaska.

What is your favorite holiday? Write about it below.

_____

History is the story of people and events from other times and places.

A **fact** is something that is true and not made up.

A **holiday** is a day when we remember and honor a special event or person.

Culture is the way a group of people live. It is made up of their special food, music, and art.

Character is used to describe someone who is honest, brave, or responsible.

Fiction is something that is not true.

Many people eat foods from different cultures. Write about a special food you eat.

_____

Draw a picture of someone who shows good character.

Write another example of fiction on the blank line.
People can fly like birds.
Money grows on trees.

6

Common Core Standards RI.4: Ask and answer questions to help determine or clarify the meaning of words and phrases in a text.

Words to Know
Active Teaching

FOLDABLES®

1. Go to connected.mcgraw-hill.com for flashcards to introduce the unit vocabulary to students.

2. Read the words on the list on page 6 and have students repeat them after you.

3. Guide students as they complete steps 1 through 4 of the Foldable activity.

4. Have students use the Foldable to practice the vocabulary words independently or with a partner.

networks

Go to connected.mcgraw-hill.com for additional resources:
- Vocabulary Flashcards
- Vocabulary Games
- Graphic Organizers

GO Vocabulary!

Use the graphic organizer below to help students gain a deeper understanding of each vocabulary word. Model for students how to complete the graphic organizer using the word *history*. Have students complete the graphic organizer for the other words independently.

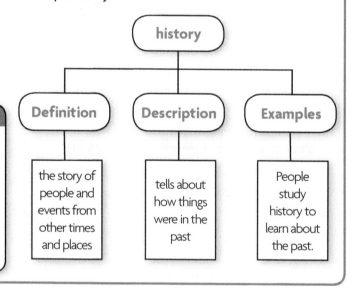

history

Definition	Description	Examples
the story of people and events from other times and places	tells about how things were in the past	People study history to learn about the past.

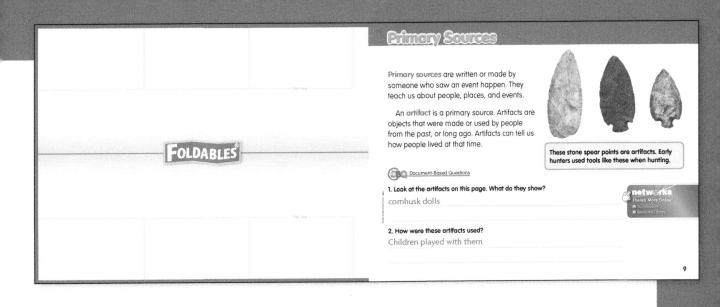

Primary Sources

Primary sources are written or made by someone who saw an event happen. They teach us about people, places, and events.

An **artifact** is a primary source. Artifacts are objects that were made or used by people from the past, or long ago. Artifacts can tell us how people lived at that time.

These stone spear points are artifacts. Early hunters used tools like these when hunting.

DBQ Document-Based Questions

1. Look at the artifacts on this page. What do they show?

cornhusk dolls

2. How were these artifacts used?

Children played with them.

9

Differentiated Instruction

▶ **ELL** Act out or provide visuals of each word with students. For example, for the word *holiday*, act like you are celebrating by waving an American flag. Point to the flag and say, *"It is July 4TH. We are celebrating a holiday."* Have students repeat the word *holiday*. Have students describe a time when they celebrated a holiday. Repeat the activity with the words *history, fact, community, time line, technology, slavery, culture, character, tall tale, fable, fiction,* and *nonfiction*.

W O R D P L A Y

Matching/Concentration

Create matching cards that illustrate the unit vocabulary. After cards are matched, students can play the memory game "Concentration" and keep the pairs which they correctly match when they turn over two cards on their turn.

netw⊙rks

Go to connected.mcgraw-hill.com for additional resources:
• Skill Builders   • Resource Library

Primary Sources
Active Teaching

Use page 9 to teach your students about using artifacts to learn about how people may have lived long ago. Read the page together. Discuss the picture of the artifact on page 9. Guide students through the written activities.

Develop Comprehension
Ask:

1. *How can artifacts help us understand what life was like long ago?* (they are from the past) **L2**

2. *How are artifacts the same or different from someone's written description of life long ago?* **L3**

Clarify Misconceptions

Students may think that all old objects are artifacts. Inform students that some artifacts could be recreated or made or altered with technology. Tell students that historians examine primary source artifacts carefully to ensure that what they portray and what time period they are from is authentic.

More About Primary Sources Many primary sources are part of the Library of Congress collection. To view more of their collection, visit www.memory.loc.gov/ammem/. This Web site provides over 7 million historical documents, photos, images, films, and audio recordings.

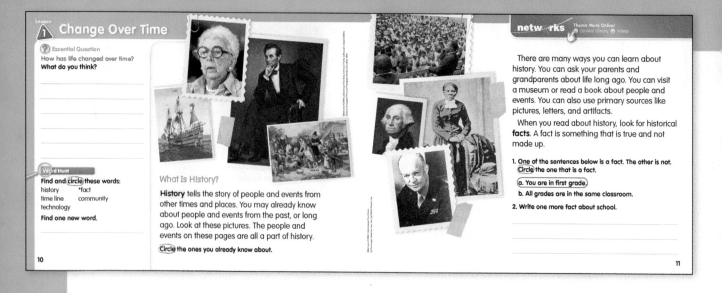

Activate Prior Knowledge

Engage students in a discussion about memories they have of when they were little. Tell students that things that have happened in the past are a part of our history.

Ask: *What do you know about history? What examples of your family history can you give?*

Explain that in this lesson, students will learn that history tells the story of people and events of long ago.

? Essential Question How has life changed over time?

Have students explain what they understand about the Essential Question. Discuss their responses. Explain that everything they learn in this lesson will help them understand the Essential Question better. Remind them to think about how the Essential Question connects to the unit Big Idea: People and events shape history.

Differentiated Instruction

▶ **Approaching** Have students look at the illustrations on pages 10–11.

Ask: *What makes something a part of history?*

▶ **Beyond** Instruct students to pick one of the historical figures shown on page 10 and write a paragraph or bulleted list of historical facts about the person. Ask them to share with the class.

▶ **ELL** Write the word *history* on the board. Explain how anything that has happened in the past is part of history. Have students share something from their own family history.

Active Teaching

Words To Know In each lesson, students will be learning both content and academic vocabulary. Academic vocabulary words are marked with an asterisk (*) on the lesson opener and are boldface within the text.

Have students look through the lesson to find the words that are listed in the Word Hunt. Then have them read the definitions of content vocabulary words and use context clues or the glossary to determine the meanings of the academic vocabulary words.

Define the academic vocabulary word *fact* for students. Ask students to give you an example of a fact.

Develop Comprehension

As students read the spread, use these questions to develop comprehension.

1. *Why is history important?* (to learn about the past) **L3**
2. *What is a fact?* (something that is true) **L1**
3. *Who can teach us about our family history?* (grandparents, parents, siblings, etc.) **L2**

Family Life Then

Long ago, families lived in one-room cabins without electricity or running water. They used candles and oil lamps to see in the dark. They cooked their meals over an open fire.

Children had chores like they do today. Most of the time, children would do their chores before and after school. For many children, that meant helping out on the farm.

For fun, girls played games like hopscotch. They also played with cornhusk dolls. Boys played with jacks or marbles.

> Underline four facts that describe family life in the past.

Family Life Now

Today, our homes have electricity and running water. We cook meals in ovens and store food in refrigerators.

Children still do many of the same things they did long ago. They go to school and play games. They also have chores. But today, some children get money for doing their chores.

Children still play games today. Games are much different from long ago. Today, children play video or computer games.

> Draw a picture of your home.

Media Center

Use the Internet and other sources to find out:

1. What chores did children do long ago compared to today?

2. What games do children play now that they didn't have in the past?

Active Teaching

Read and discuss pages 12 and 13 together. Guide students as they complete the activities.

Develop Comprehension

Ask:

1. *What games did children play long ago?* (hopscotch, marbles, jacks) **L1**

2. *What games are played today?* (computer and video games) **L1**

3. *What is the difference between homes long ago and today?* (Many homes long ago had only one room and did not have electricity or running water; homes today have multiple rooms and stories and have electricity, gas, and running water.) **L2**

FUN FACT

Say: *An early American version of jacks was known as jack-stones. Children actually used stones or pebbles instead of marbles. As time went on, the pebbles were replaced by rubber balls and the jacks became metal-pointed objects.*

☑ Formative Assessment

Have students summarize what they have learned about families long ago and today. Ask them to write down two facts that they have learned.

Differentiated Instruction

▶ **Approaching** Invite students to bring in old family photos. Display the photos and have students describe how people's lives have changed.

▶ **Beyond** Ask children to use the Internet to locate photos showing home life long ago. Then have them write a caption for each photo.

▶ **ELL** Have students ask about their family's past by talking to parents, grandparents, etc. Have them ask at least 3 questions of someone in their native language. Then have them work with a partner in the class to help translate their text.

Media Center Have students work in groups to use the media center to research other things that are from long ago. Make sure they research things used in family life, homes, school, work, and communities. Have each group pick a topic and create a "then and now" poster with at least 2 sentences under each heading. Then have each group share with the class.

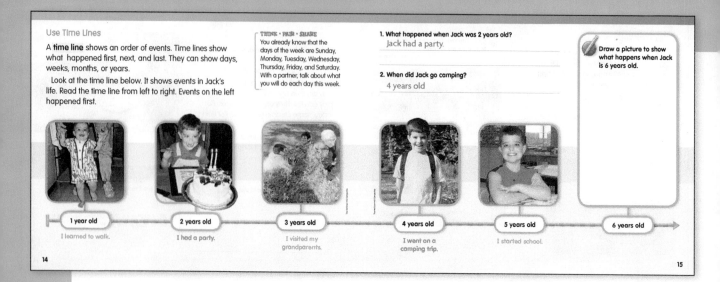

A **time line** shows an order of events. Time lines show what happened first, next, and last. They can show days, weeks, months, or years.

Look at the time line below. It shows events in Jack's life. Read the time line from left to right. Events on the left happened first.

THINK • PAIR • SHARE
You already know that the days of the week are Sunday, Monday, Tuesday, Wednesday, Thursday, Friday, and Saturday. With a partner, talk about what you will do each day this week.

1. What happened when Jack was 2 years old?
Jack had a party.

2. When did Jack go camping?
4 years old

Draw a picture to show what happens when Jack is 6 years old.

1 year old	2 years old	3 years old	4 years old	5 years old	6 years old
I learned to walk.	I had a party.	I visited my grandparents.	I went on a camping trip.	I started school.	

14

15

Lesson 1

Active Teaching

Words To Know Write the words *time line* on the board. Tell students that a time line is a chart with pictures, dates, and time words arranged on a line. Point out that with a time line, you can show the order of events. Explain that an event is something of importance that happens. A time line also gives information about the events.

Develop Comprehension

Ask:

1. *What can you learn from a time line?* (You can learn information about events and the order in which they happened.) **L2**

2. *What happened when Jack was 1 year old?* (He learned to walk.) **L1**

3. *Which event happened 3rd in Jack's life, according to the time line?* (Jack visited his grandparents.) **L2**

Differentiated Instruction

▶ **Approaching** Have students think of three events that have happened today. Ask them to write them down in sequential order on a time line and draw a picture for each item.

▶ **Beyond** Ask students to create a time line of their own life from birth to the present. Have them include at least four events. They should have a sentence for each year they list and either a photograph or an illustration for each event.

▶ **ELL** Have students bring in photographs of their life and put them on a piece of paper in order. Then ask them to explain what each photograph shows.

✓ Formative Assessment

Ask students to think about what they do at each time of the day. Have them create a time line of their own. They should label it with the words *morning, afternoon,* and *evening*. Write sample responses in order on the time line on the board. Have pairs exchange their work and take turns explaining each other's time lines.

School Then

Imagine going to school in a single room with much older kids. That's right! A long time ago, one teacher taught all students. The older kids would sometimes help teach the younger ones.

Students learned how to write on slates, or small chalkboards. They learned how to read using a hornbook. A hornbook is a piece of wood with a sheet of paper attached to it. The paper usually had the alphabet written on it.

Reading Skill

Finding Similarities and Differences **Look at the picture of the hornbook. How is it the same as the books you read? How is it different?**

Same:
has letters and pictures on it

Different:
on a piece of wood, can't turn the pages, only 1 page

16

School Now

Today, schools are bigger than they were long ago. Students go to school in buildings with many rooms. Most classes have their own classroom.

Schools have many tools to help students learn. Some classrooms have computers, TVs, and whiteboards. Many schools also have a computer lab and a library.

 Draw a picture of your school.

1. What were classrooms like in the past?

2. What are classrooms like today?

17

Active Teaching

Read and discuss pages 16 and 17 as a class. Guide students as they complete the activities.

Ask: *How are schools today different from long ago?*

Explain that by understanding more about history, we may understand how things have changed.

Develop Comprehension

1. *What did students use to read long ago?* (hornbook) **L1**

2. *How are school buildings today different from long ago?* (one room building vs. multiple rooms) **L2**

3. *What kind of tools are used in today's classrooms that were not used long ago?* (computers, TVs, whiteboards) **L1**

☑ Formative Assessment

Have students summarize what they know about schools long ago. Have them draw a picture or write a brief description. Use this assessment to monitor student understanding and identify need for intervention.

Differentiated Instruction

▶ **Approaching** Divide the class into two groups. Have one group role play that they are in a school from the past for one day. Have the other group use modern equipment and act normally. Reverse roles. Have students describe the differences afterwards.

▶ **Beyond** Ask students to write a few sentences on how they would feel if they had to attend a one-room school house from long ago. Have them draw a picture to go along with their story.

▶ **ELL** Ask students to think of how schools have changed over time in their native country. Share with the class.

Reading Skill

Common Core Standards RI.9: Identify basic similarities and differences between two texts on the same topic (e.g. in illustrations, descriptions, and procedures).

Finding Similarities and Differences Have students read the text on pages 16–17 and place things that are alike and different in a Venn diagram graphic organizer.

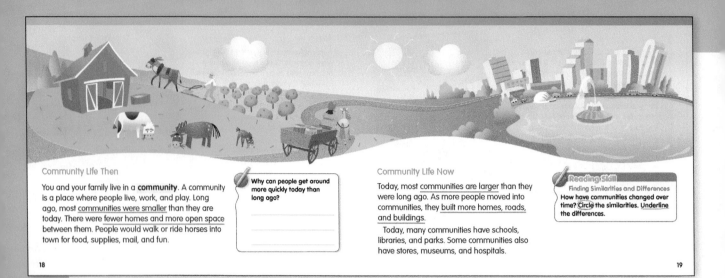

Community Life Then

You and your family live in a **community**. A community is a place where people live, work, and play. Long ago, most communities were smaller than they are today. There were fewer homes and more open space between them. People would walk or ride horses into town for food, supplies, mail, and fun.

Why can people get around more quickly today than long ago?

_____

_____

18

Community Life Now

Today, most communities are larger than they were long ago. As more people moved into communities, they built more homes, roads, and buildings.

Today, many communities have schools, libraries, and parks. Some communities also have stores, museums, and hospitals.

Reading Skill
Finding Similarities and Differences
How have communities changed over time? Circle the similarities. Underline the differences.

19

Lesson 1

Active Teaching

As they read, remind students to compare life now with life in the past. Read and discuss page 18.

Ask: *How were communities different in the past compared to how they are today?*

Explain that by understanding more about history, we may understand how things have changed.

Develop Comprehension

1. *What is a community?* (a place where people live, work, and play) **L1**

2. *How are communities today different from long ago?* (They were usually a lot smaller compared to today.) **L2**

3. *How did people get to town long ago?* (walked or rode horses) **L1**

☑ Formative Assessment

Have students summarize what they know about communities long ago. Have them draw a picture or write a brief description. Use this assessment to monitor student understanding and identify need for intervention.

Differentiated Instruction

▶ **Approaching** Divide the class into two groups. Have one group role play that they are in a community from the past for one day. Have the other group use modern equipment and act normally. Reverse roles. Have students describe the differences afterwards.

▶ **Beyond** Ask students to write a few sentences on how they would feel if they lived in a community from long ago. Have them draw a picture to go along with their story.

▶ **ELL** Have students discuss the images on the pages and tell how they are the same and different.

Reading Skill

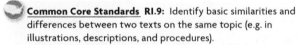

Common Core Standards RI.9: Identify basic similarities and differences between two texts on the same topic (e.g. in illustrations, descriptions, and procedures).

Finding Similarities and Differences Have students read the text on pages 18–19 and place things that are alike and different in a Venn diagram graphic organizer.

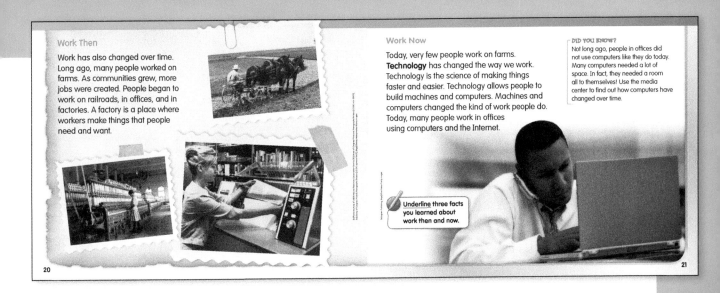

Work Then

Work has also changed over time. Long ago, many people worked on farms. As communities grew, more jobs were created. People began to work on railroads, in offices, and in factories. A factory is a place where workers make things that people need and want.

Work Now

Today, very few people work on farms. **Technology** has changed the way we work. Technology is the science of making things faster and easier. Technology allows people to build machines and computers. Machines and computers changed the kind of work people do. Today, many people work in offices using computers and the Internet.

DID YOU KNOW?

Not long ago, people in offices did not use computers like they do today. Many computers needed a lot of space. In fact, they needed a room all to themselves! Use the media center to find out how computers have changed over time.

Underline three facts you learned about work then and now.

Active Teaching

Read and discuss page 20 together.

Ask: *How is work today different from long ago?*

Divide students into groups of four. Have each group list how technology has changed over time. Share each list with the class.

Develop Comprehension

1. *What is technology?* (the science of making things faster and easier) **L1**

2. *How is work today different from long ago?* (Most people worked on farms a long time ago compared to in factories and offices today.) **L2**

3. *What technology do we use at work today?* (computers and other machines) **L2**

✓ Formative Assessment

Have students summarize what they know about work long ago. Have them draw a picture or write a brief description. Use this assessment to monitor student understanding and identify need for intervention.

Media Center Have students work in groups to use the media center to research other kinds of technology that has changed over time. Have students research things like telephones, copy machines, and other office equipment. Have each group pick a piece of technology and write at least two sentences about how it has changed and draw a picture. Then have each group share with the class.

Differentiated Instruction

▶ **Approaching** Divide the class into two groups. Have one group role play that they at work in the past for one day. Have the other group use modern equipment and pretend they are at work today. Reverse roles. Have students describe the differences afterwards.

▶ **Beyond** Ask students to write a few sentences on how they would feel if they had to work using the tools from long ago. Have them draw a picture to go along with their story.

▶ **ELL** Have students orally complete the following sentence frames about work: *Long ago, people worked _____. Today, people work _____.*

netw⊙rks

Go to connected.mcgraw-hill.com for additional resources:
- Interactive Whiteboard Activities
- Worksheets
- Assessment
- Content Library

My State on the Map
Look at the map. Color your state green. Do any other states touch your state? Color them orange.
How many states touch your state?

More to Know!
Geography

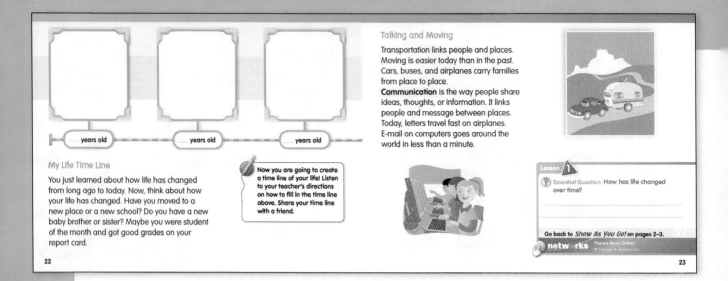

My Life Time Line

You just learned about how life has changed from long ago to today. Now, think about how your life has changed. Have you moved to a new place or a new school? Do you have a new baby brother or sister? Maybe you were student of the month and got good grades on your report card.

Now you are going to create a time line of your life! Listen to your teacher's directions on how to fill in the time line above. Share your time line with a friend.

Talking and Moving

Transportation links people and places. Moving is easier today than in the past. Cars, buses, and airplanes carry families from place to place.

Communication is the way people share ideas, thoughts, or information. It links people and message between places. Today, letters travel fast on airplanes. E-mail on computers goes around the world in less than a minute.

Lesson 1

Essential Question How has life changed over time?

Go back to *Show As You Go!* on pages 2–3.

netw rks There's More Online!

Lesson 1

Active Teaching

Have children draw a picture of something that happened to them in preschool or kindergarten. Provide them with the prompt: "*I remember when _____.*" Ask students to write or dictate a short sentence describing the event using this prompt.

Summarize the lesson with the class. Then have students respond to the Essential Question. Discuss students' responses. Have students revisit their response on page 10 and compare it to their response at the end of the lesson. Discuss how their answers changed.

> ***Show As You Go!*** Remind students to go back to the Unit Opener and complete the activities for this lesson.

Response to Intervention

? **Essential Question** **How has life changed over time?**

If . . . students cannot give a substantiated response to the Essential Question, "How has life changed over time?"

. . . .

Then . . . take students back to pages 10 through 23. Discuss how life has changed over time.

Ask: *What was family, school, community, and work life like long ago?*

Following the discussion, allow students to respond to the Essential Question again.

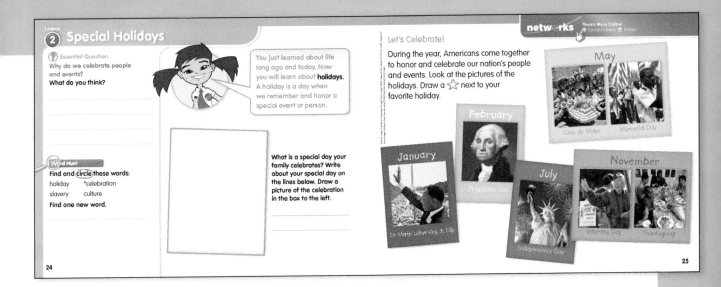

Lesson 2

Activate Prior Knowledge

Explain to students that many holidays we celebrate in our country have to do with people and events from the past. Display a calendar and ask children to name holidays in each month and tell what they know about them.

Ask: *Why do you think we celebrate holidays?*

(?) **Essential Question** **Why do we celebrate people and events?**

Have students explain what they understand about the Essential Question. Discuss their responses. Explain that everything they learn in this lesson will help them understand the Essential Question better. Remind them to think about how the Essential Question connects to the unit Big Idea: People and events shape history.

Active Teaching

Words To Know Have students look through the lesson to find the words that are listed in the Word Hunt. Then have them read the definitions of content vocabulary words and use context clues or the glossary to determine the meanings of the academic vocabulary words.

Have students find the vocabulary words in the text and read the definitions. Define the academic vocabulary word *celebrate* for students. Describe how we celebrate our holidays and traditions.

Develop Comprehension

Read and discuss the pages together. Guide students through the written activities. Discuss their responses.

Ask:

1. *Who do we remember on holidays?* (people and events) **L1**

2. *What month do we celebrate Cinco de Mayo?* (May) **L1**

3. *Name a holiday you celebrate that is not on this page.* **L2**

Differentiated Instruction

▶ **ELL** Using books or magazines, point to pictures or symbols from holidays such as July 4th and Thanksgiving Day. Mix these photos up and ask volunteers to come up and point to a holiday as you name it.

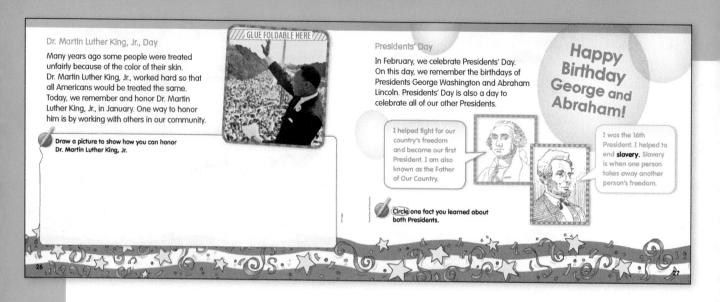

Dr. Martin Luther King, Jr., Day

Many years ago some people were treated unfairly because of the color of their skin. Dr. Martin Luther King, Jr., worked hard so that all Americans would be treated the same. Today, we remember and honor Dr. Martin Luther King, Jr., in January. One way to honor him is by working with others in our community.

Draw a picture to show how you can honor Dr. Martin Luther King, Jr.

GLUE FOLDABLE HERE

Presidents' Day

In February, we celebrate Presidents' Day. On this day, we remember the birthdays of Presidents George Washington and Abraham Lincoln. Presidents' Day is also a day to celebrate all of our other Presidents.

Happy Birthday George and Abraham!

I helped fight for our country's freedom and became our first President. I am also known as the Father of Our Country.

I was the 16th President. I helped to end **slavery**. Slavery is when one person takes away another person's freedom.

Circle one fact you learned about both Presidents.

26   27

Lesson 2

Active Teaching

Read pages 26 and 27 together. Display the month of January on the calendar in the classroom. Point to January 15 and explain that this is Martin Luther King, Jr.'s, birthday. Explain that this is why we celebrate Martin Luther King, Jr., in the month of January. Then go to February and explain that both George Washington and Abraham Lincoln had birthdays in February. Then guide students as they complete the written activities. Discuss their responses.

Develop Comprehension

Ask:

1. *How do we honor Martin Luther King, Jr.?* (working with others in our community) **L1**

2. *In what month do we celebrate Presidents' Day?* (February) **L1**

3. *What is slavery?* (when one person takes away another person's freedom) **L2**

Page Power

Interact more with the page. Have students create a Notebook Foldable to assist them in developing their understanding of important Americans.

- Provide each student with a copy of Foldable 1A from the Notebook Foldables section at the back of this book.

- Have students cut out the Foldable and glue its anchor tab on page 26 above the image.

- On the Foldable flap, have students compose a letter thanking Martin Luther King, Jr., for all that he has done for our country. Remind students to include reasons in their letter.

Differentiated Instruction

▶ **Approaching** Explain how many holidays are celebrated on the honored person's birthday or when an event happened each year. Ask students when they were born. Have them point to their birthday on the calendar.

▶ **Beyond** Tell students Martin Luther King, Jr., had a dream. Ask them if they have a dream for their family, their school, or the world. Have them draw a picture and complete the sentence, *"My dream for _____ would be _____."*

▶ **ELL** Have students name holidays that honor people in their native country. Have them point to the calendar to show when these celebrations happen. Then have them tell why each person is remembered.

netw⊕rks

Go to connected.mcgraw-hill.com for additional resources:
- Interactive Whiteboard Lessons
- Worksheets
- Assessment
- Videos

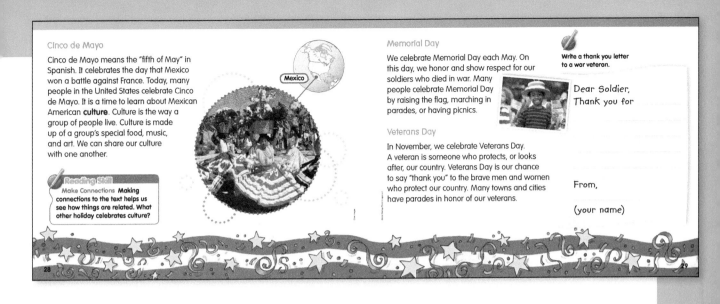

Cinco de Mayo

Cinco de Mayo means the "fifth of May" in Spanish. It celebrates the day that Mexico won a battle against France. Today, many people in the United States celebrate Cinco de Mayo. It is a time to learn about Mexican American **culture**. Culture is the way a group of people live. Culture is made up of a group's special food, music, and art. We can share our culture with one another.

Reading Skill

Make Connections Making connections to the text helps us see how things are related. What other holiday celebrates culture?

Memorial Day

We celebrate Memorial Day each May. On this day, we honor and show respect for our soldiers who died in war. Many people celebrate Memorial Day by raising the flag, marching in parades, or having picnics.

Veterans Day

In November, we celebrate Veterans Day. A veteran is someone who protects, or looks after, our country. Veterans Day is our chance to say "thank you" to the brave men and women who protect our country. Many towns and cities have parades in honor of our veterans.

Write a thank you letter to a war veteran.

Dear Soldier,
Thank you for

From,

(your name)

28

29

Active Teaching

Read pages 28 and 29 together. Display a calendar in the classroom. Go to the month of May. Point to May 5th and the last Monday in May. Explain what holidays are celebrated on these days (Cinco de Mayo and Memorial Day). Do the same thing with November 11th and Veterans Day. Then guide students as they complete the written activities. Discuss their responses.

Develop Comprehension

Ask:

1. *When is Cinco de Mayo celebrated?* (May 5th) **L1**

2. *In what month do we celebrate Veterans Day?* (November) **L1**

3. *What is culture?* (the way a group of people live) **L2**

✔ Formative Assessment

Have students list an important holiday that they have learned about so far and write three facts about it. Then ask them to draw a picture depicting this holiday and share with the class.

DID YOU KNOW?

Discuss why Cinco de Mayo is an important holiday to Mexicans and Mexican Americans. Explain that the holiday is celebrated in honor of Mexican freedom. On May 5, 1862, French troops attacked the city of Puebla, Mexico. The Mexican army was much smaller than the French army, but they won the battle in less than four hours.

Differentiated Instruction

▶ **Approaching** Discuss what a veteran is. Explain to students that on Veterans Day, we celebrate those who have served our country in the armed services. Tell students that Memorial Day honors veterans who have died.

▶ **Beyond** Have students research and interview a local veteran in their community. It can be a neighbor, family, or friend. Have the students ask three questions of this person. Then have them share the person's responses with the class.

▶ **ELL** Ask students how veterans are celebrated in their country. Ask them to draw a picture showing this.

Reading Skill

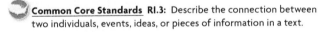 **Common Core Standards RI.3:** Describe the connection between two individuals, events, ideas, or pieces of information in a text.

Make Connections Have students read the text on pages 28–29. Ask them think of another holiday their family may celebrate.

Independence Day

A long time ago, America belonged to another country. America's leaders met in 1776 to sign the Declaration of Independence. This important paper said that America wanted to be free.

Thomas Jefferson and Benjamin Franklin were two of these brave leaders. Thanks to them and others, we now celebrate our independence. The Fourth of July is the birthday of our country. It is also called Independence Day.

Many people wave our flag on this day. Do you know what the colors of our flag stand for? The red stands for courage. The white stands for purity, or goodness. The blue stands for loyalty.

Create your own classroom flag to the right. Make sure it has many colors and shapes!

Thanksgiving Day

A long time ago, Pilgrims came to live in America. Their lives were very hard. They had trouble growing enough food. A group of Native Americans helped the Pilgrims. They showed the Pilgrims how to grow new crops. The Pilgrims wanted to thank the Native Americans for their help. They invited the Native Americans for a special meal. This day became known as Thanksgiving Day.

DID YOU KNOW?
In 1863, President Abraham Lincoln made Thanksgiving Day a national holiday. We now celebrate Thanksgiving on the last Thursday in November every year.

Lesson 2

? Essential Question Why do we celebrate people and events?

Go back to *Show As You Go!* on pages 2–3.

networks There's More Online! Games Assessment

30

31

Lesson 2

Active Teaching

Read and discuss pages 30 and 31 together. Guide students as they complete the written activities, except for the Essential Question.

Develop Comprehension

Ask:

1. *Why do we celebrate Independence Day?* (to recognize our country's freedom) **L3**

2. *Who made Thanksgiving a national holiday?* (Abraham Lincoln) **L2**

3. *How did the Pilgrims give thanks to the Native Americans?* (The Pilgrims invited the Native Americans to a feast.) **L2**

Summarize the lesson with the class. Then have students respond to the Essential Question. Discuss students' responses. Have students revisit their response on page 24 and compare it to their response at the end of the lesson. Discuss how their answers changed.

Use the leveled reader, *The First Thanksgiving,* to extend and enrich students' understanding of celebrations and holidays. A lesson plan for this leveled reader can be found on pages T16–T17 at the front of this Teacher Edition.

> ***Show As You Go!*** Remind students to go back to the Unit Opener and complete the activities for this lesson.

Response to Intervention

? **Essential Question** **Why do we celebrate people and events?**

If . . . students cannot give a substantiated response to the Essential Question, "Why do we celebrate people and events?"

. . . .

Then . . . write the name of each holiday from Lesson 2 in each row of a chart. Discuss with students the importance of each holiday and why they are important for us to celebrate. List students' responses on the chart.

Ask: *What holidays do you celebrate to help you remember the past?*

Following the discussion, allow students to respond to the Essential Question again.

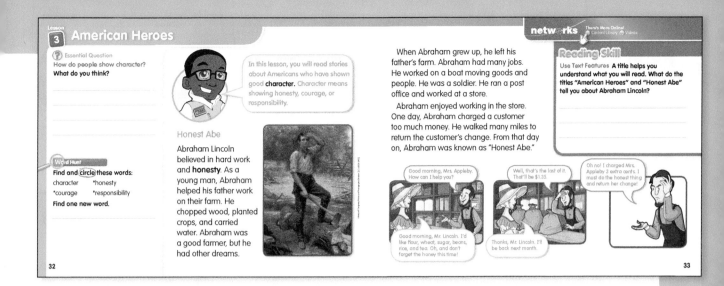

Lesson 3

Activate Prior Knowledge

Gather the students around you. Hold up a five-dollar bill (or something similar).

Say: *I found this money in the hallway today. I don't know who it belongs to. I wonder what I should do with it. What would you do?*

As students give you suggestions, write them on the board. If students say that they would turn in the money to a teacher, mention that that would be honest. Tell them that if they kept the money for themselves that that wouldn't be honest or right.

Explain to students that in this lesson, they will be learning about people from the past who have shown good character ideals and principles.

? Essential Question How do people show character?

Have students explain what they understand about the Essential Question. Discuss their responses. Explain that everything they learn in this lesson will help them understand the Essential Question better. Remind them to think about how the Essential Question connects to the unit Big Idea: People and events shape history.

Reading Skill

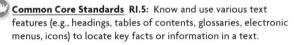

Common Core Standards RI.5: Know and use various text features (e.g., headings, tables of contents, glossaries, electronic menus, icons) to locate key facts or information in a text.

Use Text Features For additional practice, ask students to underline the words in the text that help them understand what "Honest Abe" means.

Active Teaching

Words To Know Have students look through the lesson to find the words that are listed in the Word Hunt. Then have them read the definitions of content vocabulary words and use context clues or the glossary to determine the meanings of the academic vocabulary words.

Define the academic vocabulary word *courage* for students. Describe how courage shows people how brave we are in difficult situations.

Develop Comprehension

Read and discuss pages 32–33 together. Guide students through the written activities. Discuss their responses.

Ask:

1. *What is character?* (traits that describe people as honest, brave, or responsible) **L1**

2. *What jobs did Abraham Lincoln have growing up?* (farmer, worked on a boat, soldier, post office worker, and store worker) **L2**

3. *Why is it important to be honest?* (So people can trust you.) **L3**

Differentiated Instruction

▶ **ELL** Draw a concept map graphic organizer on the board and write the word *honesty* in the center. Have students describe in their own words three ways people can be honest. Record their responses on the graphic organizer. Read the graphic organizer together.

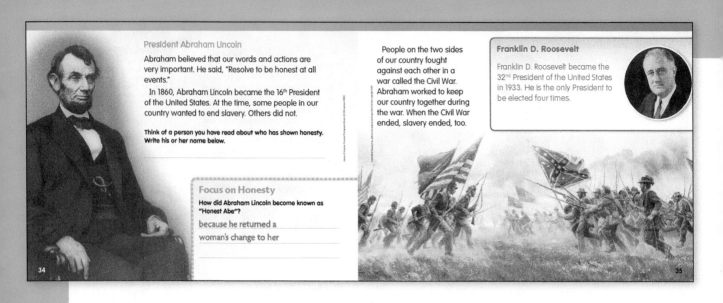

President Abraham Lincoln

Abraham believed that our words and actions are very important. He said, "Resolve to be honest at all events."

In 1860, Abraham Lincoln became the 16th President of the United States. At the time, some people in our country wanted to end slavery. Others did not.

Think of a person you have read about who has shown honesty. Write his or her name below.

Focus on Honesty

How did Abraham Lincoln become known as "Honest Abe"?

because he returned a

woman's change to her

People on the two sides of our country fought against each other in a war called the Civil War. Abraham worked to keep our country together during the war. When the Civil War ended, slavery ended, too.

Franklin D. Roosevelt

Franklin D. Roosevelt became the 32nd President of the United States in 1933. He is the only President to be elected four times.

34   35

Lesson 3

Active Teaching

Read pages 34 and 35 together. Have partners discuss how each person showed character. Guide students through the written activities.

Develop Comprehension

Ask:

1. *Why did Abraham Lincoln act like he did?* (He believed words and actions are very important.) **L3**

2. *What ended when the Civil War ended?* (slavery) **L2**

3. *Who became President in 1933?* (Franklin D. Roosevelt) **L1**

✔ Formative Assessment

List each person discussed in this lesson and their character traits on separate index cards. Have students match each person to their trait. Then have students explain why each person was important to our country.

More About...Abraham Lincoln Abraham Lincoln was also a lawyer. He made the quote on page 34 during a speech as a lawyer. Why do you think his quote is important? Why is it important to have honesty when someone is a lawyer? Why is it important for a President to be honest?

Differentiated Instruction

▶ **Approaching** Encourage students to tell you about a time when they saw someone do something that was not honest. Ask them to tell you how they would act honestly in the same situation.

▶ **Beyond** Discuss different ways that people can be dishonest, such as lying, cheating on a test, or taking something that isn't theirs. Have students make pictures that illustrate the "do's and dont's" in these different situations. Encourage them to write a sentence about each situation.

▶ **ELL** Have a volunteer come up and drop a personal item.

    Say: *Look! I found this. I'm going to keep it.*

    Ask: *Is this mine? Can I keep it?*

Ask students to answer your questions. Encourage volunteers to come up and repeat the scenario.

Harriet Tubman's Courage

Harriet Tubman was born in Maryland around 1820. She was born into slavery. People in slavery worked long hours with little rest. They could not go to school or make their own choices.

Harriet heard about something called the Underground Railroad. The Underground Railroad was not a train.

Frederick Douglass also helped the Underground Railroad. He had learned to read early in his life and wrote many books on his journey to freedom.

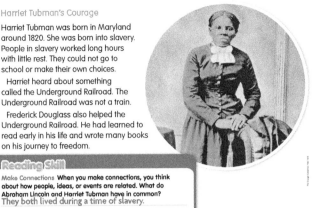

Reading Skill

Make Connections When you make connections, you think about how people, ideas, or events are related. What do Abraham Lincoln and Harriet Tubman have in common? They both lived during a time of slavery.

36

The Underground Railroad was a group of people who helped others in slavery escape, or run away. The Underground Railroad gave people food and a place to rest until they reached a place that did not have slavery.

In 1849 Harriet ran away to Pennsylvania. She was finally free. Harriet wanted to help others find freedom. This meant she had to risk her own life. Harriet joined the Underground Railroad and helped many people escape slavery. Today, we remember Harriet Tubman for her **courage**.

Focus on Courage

Write about someone you know who has shown courage.

37

Active Teaching

Read and discuss pages 36 and 37 together. Guide students through the written activities. Explain that courage means to act bravely.

Ask: *Who do you know that has courage?*

Develop Comprehension

Ask:

1. *What was the Underground Railroad?* (a group of people who helped others in slavery escape) **L2**

2. *What does* courage *mean?* (to act bravely) **L1**

3. *What is Harriet Tubman remembered for?* (courage and helping the Underground Railroad) **L2**

Use the leveled reader, *Daniel Inouye*, to extend and enrich students' understanding of another hero in history. A lesson plan for this leveled reader can be found on pages T18–T19 at the front of this Teacher Edition.

Reading Skill

Common Core Standards RI.3: Describe the connection between two individuals, events, ideas, or pieces of information in a text.

Make Connections For additional practice, ask students to underline the connections between Abraham Lincoln and Harriet Tubman in each paragraph of the lesson.

Differentiated Instruction

▶ **Approaching** Encourage students to tell you about a time when they had a lot of courage. It might be going to a new school, making a new friend, or taking a test.

▶ **Beyond** Write a short paragraph explaining why Harriet Tubman was courageous.

▶ **ELL** Ask students to describe what freedom means in their native country. Ask them to work in pairs and share their stories.

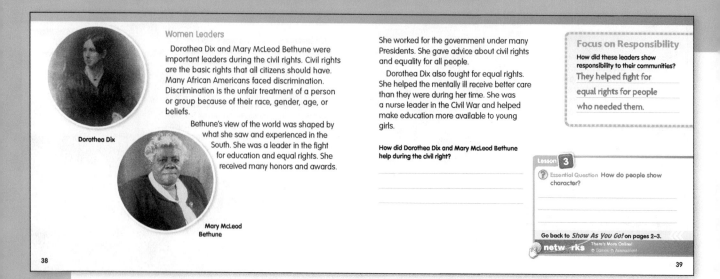

Women Leaders

Dorothea Dix and Mary McLeod Bethune were important leaders during the civil rights. Civil rights are the basic rights that all citizens should have. Many African Americans faced discrimination. Discrimination is the unfair treatment of a person or group because of their race, gender, age, or beliefs.

Bethune's view of the world was shaped by what she saw and experienced in the South. She was a leader in the fight for education and equal rights. She received many honors and awards.

Dorothea Dix

Mary McLeod Bethune

She worked for the government under many Presidents. She gave advice about civil rights and equality for all people.

Dorothea Dix also fought for equal rights. She helped the mentally ill receive better care than they were during her time. She was a nurse leader in the Civil War and helped make education more available to young girls.

How did Dorothea Dix and Mary McLeod Bethune help during the civil right?

_____

_____

_____

Focus on Responsibility

How did these leaders show responsibility to their communities?

They helped fight for

equal rights for people

who needed them.

Lesson 3

Essential Question How do people show character?

_____

_____

Go back to *Show As You Go!* on pages 2–3.

netw⚡rks There's More Online!

38

39

Lesson 3

Active Teaching

Read and discuss pages 38 and 39 together. Guide students as they complete the written activities, except for the Essential Question.

Develop Comprehension

Ask:

1. *What are civil rights?* (rights all citizens have) **L1**

2. *What did Dorothea Dix do in the Civil War?* (she was a nurse) **L1**

3. *Who did Mary McLeod Bethune fight for?* **L2**

Summarize the lesson with the class. Then have students respond to the Essential Question. Discuss students' responses. Have students revisit their response on page 32 and compare it to their response at the end of the lesson. Discuss how their answers changed.

Use the leveled reader, *Coretta Scott King*, to extend and enrich students' understanding of people showing responsibility. A lesson plan for this leveled reader can be found on pages T20–T21 at the front of this Teacher Edition.

Show As You Go! Remind students to go back to the Unit Opener and complete the activities for this lesson.

Response to Intervention

❓ **Essential Question How do people show character?**

If . . . students cannot give a substantiated response to the Essential Question, "How do people show character?"

· ·

Then . . . write the name of each character trait they learned about in Lesson 3 on the board. Discuss with students the importance of each character trait they named.

Ask: *How do people show they are brave, honest, or responsible?*

Following the discussion, allow students to respond to the Essential Question again.

Activate Prior Knowledge

Engage students in a discussion about stories.

Ask: *Are all stories about a real person or event? How do you know? Where do old stories come from?*

Explain that in this lesson, students will learn about why we read stories and where they come from.

(?) **Essential Question** **Why do we read stories?**

Have students explain what they understand about the Essential Question. Discuss their responses. Explain that everything they learn in this lesson will help them understand the Essential Question better. Remind them to think about how the Essential Question connects to the unit Big Idea: People and events shape history.

Active Teaching

Words To Know Have students look through the lesson to find the words that are listed in the Word Hunt. Then have them read the definitions of content vocabulary words and use context clues or the glossary to determine the meanings of the academic vocabulary word.

Develop Comprehension

Read and discuss pages 40–41 together. Guide students through the written activities. Discuss their responses.

Ask:

1. *What is a tall tale?* (A story that exaggerates details.) **L1**

2. *What did Paul Bunyan do for a living?* (He was a lumberjack.) **L2**

3. *What details are exaggerated on page 41?* (that he was more than 50 feet tall; that he could cut down more than 100 trees with one swing) **L3**

Differentiated Instruction

▶ **ELL** Reread the sentences where the vocabulary words appear in the lesson. Then have students explain what the vocabulary words mean in their own words.

Paul had a loyal friend named Babe. <u>Babe was a blue ox</u>. Some people say <u>Babe was as big as a mountain</u>. Babe followed Paul wherever he traveled.

42

Underline the details that tell you this story is a tall tale.

One hot summer day, Paul and Babe <u>cleared an entire forest</u>. Paul wanted to reward Babe with a fountain of water. He began to dig deep holes into the soil, looking for water. <u>Paul dug so deep that the holes became the Great Lakes!</u>

43

Lesson 4

Active Teaching

Read pages 42 and 43 together. Have partners discuss what parts of the story are make-believe (or fiction). Guide students as they complete the activities.

Develop Comprehension

Ask:

1. *What kind of animal is Babe?* (a blue ox) **L1**

2. *Why did Paul want to reward Babe?* (for helping Paul clear an entire forest) **L2**

3. *What was the weather like when they cleared the forest?* (hot summer) **L2**

Reading Skill

Common Core Standards **RI.5:** Know and use various text features (e.g. headings, tables of contents, glossaries, electronic menus, icons) to locate key facts or information in a text.

Clarify Words and Phrases For additional practice, ask students to underline words or phrases that they don't understand or know about in the lesson. Discuss with them how they can use the words they know and pictures on the page to help them figure out the words they don't know.

Differentiated Instruction

▶ **Approaching** Play a game where you read a sentence from a story and the students determine if the details are exaggerated or not.

▶ **Beyond** Have students write their own exaggerated sentences and share with a partner.

▶ **ELL** Have students point to the pictures on pages 42 and 43 that show exaggeration.

netw@rks

Go to **connected.mcgraw-hill.com** for additional resources:

- Interactive Whiteboard Lessons
- Worksheets
- Assessment
- Skill Builders

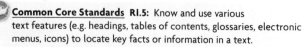

FABLES

Have you ever read a **fable**? A fable is a story that teaches a lesson. Fables often use animals or other things that talk and act like people. As you read this fable, think about who or what talks and acts like a person.

44

THE WIND AND THE SUN

One day the wind and the sun were fighting over who was stronger. "I can pull out trees by their roots and make homes shake with fear," said Wind.

"I light up the world," said Sun.

Just then, they saw a man walking down a long road. Sun had a thought. "Let's see who can make the man take off his coat. You can go first." Then Sun hid behind a cloud.

> **What two things are acting like people?**
>
> The Wind and the Sun.

45

Active Teaching

Read pages 44 and 45 together with the class. Direct their attention to the picture shown on these pages.

Ask: *Do you think this picture shows a real or make-believe scene? How can you tell?*

Develop Comprehension

Ask:

1. *What is a fable?* (a story that teaches a lesson) **L1**

2. *What were the wind and the sun fighting over?* (who was stronger) **L2**

3. *Who went first to see who was stronger?* (the wind) **L2**

Reading Skill

 Common Core Standards **RI.9:** Identify basic similarities and differences between two texts on the same topic (e.g., in illustrations, descriptions, and procedures).

Finding Similarities and Differences For additional practice, have students determine how the wind and sun are similar and different. Create a Venn diagram and complete it as a class.

Differentiated Instruction

▶ **Approaching** Encourage students to tell you about stories they have heard or read that have animals acting like people.

▶ **Beyond** Write a short paragraph explaining how the wind and the sun are acting like people

▶ **ELL** Ask students to describe what stories they know from their native country. Have them share in pairs.

Wind blew a strong gust of air, shaking all the trees in the forest. But this didn't stop the man. <u>He frowned at the wind and kept walking.</u>

Then, Wind blew heavier and stronger gusts of air. The man found it very hard to walk, but <u>he held on tight to his coat.</u> After a long while, Wind gave up.

> Underline what happened to the man when Wind had his turn.

46

Then, it was Sun's turn. Sun began to shine her rays of light through the forest. Warm rays of light shined through the trees. The animals ran out of their shelters and were happy again. The man started to whistle as he walked. Then, he took off his coat.

What is the moral, or lesson, of the story? Write your answer below.

Kindness is better than harshness.

Reading Skill

Clarify Words and Phrases
Circle the clues that help you understand the phrase "rays of light." Then write what you think it means below.

47

Lesson 4

Active Teaching

Read pages 46 and 47 together with the class. Direct their attention to the pictures on these pages.

Ask: *Do you think the wind or the sun is stronger? Why do you think this?*

Develop Comprehension

Ask:

1. *What did the wind do after it blew its first strong gust of air?* (The wind blew heavier and stronger gusts of air.) **L1**

2. *Why did the wind give up?* (The man was not taking off his coat no matter how strong the wind blew.) **L2**

3. *Why do you think the animals were happy again after the sun shined?* (The sun warmed them up.) **L2**

Reading Skill

 Common Core Standards RI.4: Ask and answer questions to help determine or clarify the meaning of words and phrases in a text.

Clarify Words and Phrases For additional practice, reread the text together to find other confusing phrases and write them on the board. Then discuss as a class to figure out what the phrases mean.

Differentiated Instruction

▶ **Approaching** Reread the story about the wind and the sun with students. After each paragraph, discuss each character's reaction to showing their strength. Then have the students state why they thought the wind or the sun should win.

▶ **Beyond** Have students read more about fables in the Content Library at connected.mcgraw-hill.com and in trade books. Have students share their favorite fable with the rest of the class.

▶ **ELL** Ask students to circle the key words in the story that show the sun's kindness. Then have them underline the words that show the wind's harshness.

Fiction or Nonfiction

Fiction or Nonfiction

The tall tale and fable you just read are **fiction**. Fiction is something that is not true. Not everything you read is fiction! Some stories are **nonfiction**. Nonfiction tells about something that is true. Is the article below fiction or nonfiction?

When I grow up....

Abby lives in sunny California. When Abby grows up, she wants to be a meteorologist. A meteorologist reports the weather. Abby likes sunny days because she can go to the beach. On rainy days, she likes to look for rainbows. The only kind of weather Abby doesn't like is the Santa Ana winds!

48

With many historical stories, some of what we read is fact and some is fiction. In Lesson 1, you learned that a fact is something that is true and not made up. In this lesson, you read stories that are fiction, or not true.

Read the sentences below. Circle fact or fiction for each sentence.

1. People can be more than 50 feet tall!

   Fact   (Fiction)

2. The sun and the wind can talk.

   Fact   (Fiction)

3. A meteorologist reports the weather.

   (Fact)   Fiction

Fact = true
Fiction = not true

Lesson 4

? Essential Question Why do we read stories?

_____

_____

_____

Go back to *Show As You Go!* **on pages 2–3.**

netw⚙rks There's More Online!
⊕ Games ⊕ Assessment

49

Active Teaching

Read pages 48 and 49 together. Ask students to describe a story they have read that was true. Ask students to then describe a story that was not true.

Develop Comprehension

Ask:

1. *Are nonfiction stories based on fact or fiction?* (fact) **L2**

2. *Are tall tales fact or fiction?* (fiction) **L1**

3. *Why is it important to read nonfiction stories?* (to learn facts and the truth about things) **L1**

Summarize the lesson with the class. Then have students respond to the Essential Question. Discuss students' responses. Have students revisit their response on page 40 and compare it to their response at the end of the lesson. Discuss how their answers changed.

> ***Show As You Go!*** Remind students to go back to complete the project on the Unit Opener.

Response to Intervention

? Essential Question **Why do we read stories?**

If . . . students cannot give a substantiated response to the Essential Question, "Why do we read stories?"

. . . .

Then . . . write the names of each kind of story the students learned about in this lesson (tall tales, fables, fiction, and nonfiction) in a chart. Have them list the characteristics of each kind of story under each column.

Ask: *How are these stories similar? Different? Explain in your own words.*

Following the discussion, allow students to respond to the Essential Question again.

Page Power

Interact more with the page. Have students create a Notebook Foldable to assist them in developing their understanding of nonfiction text.

- Provide each student with a copy of Foldable 1B from the Notebook Foldables section at the back of this book.

- Have students cut out the Foldable and glue its anchor tab on page 48 above the picture.

- On the Foldable flap, have students write a nonfiction story about their life. It can be about what they want to be when they grow up and why they want this role.

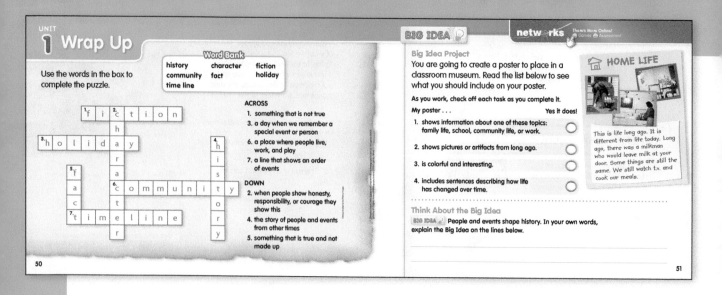

Word Bank

Use the words in the box to complete the puzzle.

history	character	fiction
community	fact	holiday
time line		

ACROSS

1. something that is not true
3. a day when we remember a special event or person
6. a place where people live, work, and play
7. a line that shows an order of events

DOWN

2. when people show honesty, responsibility, or courage they show this
4. the story of people and events from other times
5. something that is true and not made up

50

BIG IDEA

netw✺rks There's More Online! Games Assessment

Big Idea Project

You are going to create a poster to place in a classroom museum. Read the list below to see what you should include on your poster.

As you work, check off each task as you complete it.

My poster . . .   Yes it does!

1. shows information about one of these topics: family life, school, community life, or work. ◯

2. shows pictures or artifacts from long ago. ◯

3. is colorful and interesting. ◯

4. includes sentences describing how life has changed over time. ◯

Think About the Big Idea

BIG IDEA People and events shape history. In your own words, explain the Big Idea on the lines below.

🏠 HOME LIFE

This is life long ago. It is different from life today. Long ago, there was a milkman who would leave milk at your door. Some things are still the same. We still watch t.v. and cook our meals.

51

Unit 1 Wrap Up

Crossword Puzzle

Have students complete the crossword puzzle on page 50 to review the Unit 1 vocabulary.

BIG IDEA Unit Project

Students will be making a poster to show what they have learned in Unit 1. The poster will be displayed in a classroom "museum."

1. Read the checklist together and answer any questions students may have about the project.

2. Have students cut out pictures from magazines, draw their own, or bring in family pictures to create their posters. Provide supplies such as poster board, crayons, markers, magazines, scissors, and glue.

3. Have students label and briefly describe each picture on their poster.

4. Have students share their posters with the class. Then display in the classroom as a "museum." Ask what they learned from creating their posters.

5. After students complete their projects, encourage self-reflection by asking:

   • How did you choose your topic?

   • What changes would you make to this poster if you did it again?

6. To assess the project, refer to the rubric on the following page.

Differentiated Instruction

▶ **Approaching** Review the task with students. Have them write the topic on a piece of paper and find pictures that show and explain the topic long ago and today.

▶ **Beyond** Have students talk with their parents about how things in their family's past have affected their lives today. Have them include one of these events on their poster.

▶ **ELL** Have students circle key words from the checklist that they need to include on their posters. Make sure students understand the directions for the project.

Response to Intervention

BIG IDEA People and events shape history.

If . . . students cannot give a substantiated response to the Big Idea, "People and events shape history."

. . . .

Then . . . have students think about the changes that each lesson discussed. Ask students to describe the changes. Point out examples of change in each lesson—for example: How has family, school, work, and community life changed over time? Following the discussion, allow students to respond to the Big Idea again.

netw✺rks

Go to **connected.mcgraw-hill.com** for additional resources:

• Assessment
• Games
• Group Technology Projects

Name _____ Date _____

Museum Poster Rubric

4 Exemplary	3 Accomplished	2 Developing	1 Beginning
The poster:	**The poster:**	**The poster:**	**The poster:**
☐ includes all items from the task list	☐ includes most items from the task list	☐ includes several items from the task list	☐ includes few items from the task list
☐ includes multiple pictures showing life from the past	☐ includes some pictures showing life from the past	☐ includes few pictures showing life from the past	☐ does not include pictures showing life from the past
☐ is neat and organized	☐ is mostly neat and organized	☐ is somewhat neat and organized	☐ is not neat and organized
☐ contains accurate sentence descriptions for each picture	☐ has mostly accurate sentence descriptions for each picture	☐ has some accurate sentence descriptions for each picture	☐ is missing accurate sentence descriptions for each picture
☐ contains few, if any, errors in grammar, capitalization, and spelling	☐ contains some errors in grammar, capitalization, and spelling	☐ contains several errors in grammar, capitalization, and spelling	☐ contains serious errors in grammar, capitalization, and spelling

Grading Comments: _____

_____

_____

_____

_____

_____

_____

_____

_____

_____

Project Score: _____

UNIT
2 Planner WHERE WE LIVE

BIG IDEA  **Location affects how people live.**

Student Portfolio

- **Show As You Go!**
Use these pages to introduce the Big Idea. Students record information specific to each lesson. They use these pages to help them plan their Big Idea Project.

netw⊗rks

- **Group Technology Project**
Students use 21ˢᵗ century skills to complete a group extension activity of the unit project. Lesson plans, worksheets, and rubrics are available online.

Student Portfolio

- **Big Idea Project**
Students will create a community map that shows their home, school, and other places using map elements. The Big Idea Project rubric is on page 77W.

Reading Skills

Student Portfolio

- **Reading Skill: Use Visuals and Text**
Pages 54–55. Common Core State Standards RI.6, RI.7

netw⊗rks

- **Skill Builders**
Introduce and practice the reading skill.

Leveled Readers

Use the leveled reader *The Declaration of Independence* (lesson plan on T22–T23) with Lesson 2 and *On Top of the World* (lesson plan on pages T24–T25) with Lesson 3.

Treasures Connection

Teach this unit with Treasures Unit 3, *When You Mail a Letter*, pages 32–37.

Social Studies Skills

Student Portfolio

- **Primary Sources: Letter**
Page 59

netw⊗rks

- **Skill Builders**
Introduce and teach analyzing primary sources.

Activity Cards

- **Center for Social Studies Skills Investigation**
Use the center activity cards to help students explore Primary Sources, Geography, and Citizenship.

FOLDABLES®

Student Portfolio

- Students can create vocabulary Foldables right in their portfolios.
- Additional Foldables templates can be found on pages R1–R8 of your Teacher Edition.

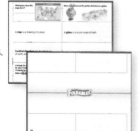

Assessment Solutions

- **McGraw-Hill networks™**
Safe online testing features multiple question types that are easy to use and editable!
- **Self-Check Quizzes**
- **Worksheets**

At a Glance

Lesson	Essential Question	Vocabulary	Digital Resources
1 Map Elements	What do maps show?	map cardinal directions compass rose map key symbol *element	Go to connected.mcgraw-hill.com for additional resources: • Interactive Whiteboard Lessons • Worksheets • Assessment • Lesson Plans • Content Library • Skill Builders • Videos • Use Standards Tracker on **networks** to track students' progress
2 Maps and Globes	What can we learn from maps and globes?	political map physical map peninsula globe *model	
3 Where We Live	How does location affect our lives?	location physical environment transportation weather seasons *affects	

*denotes academic vocabulary

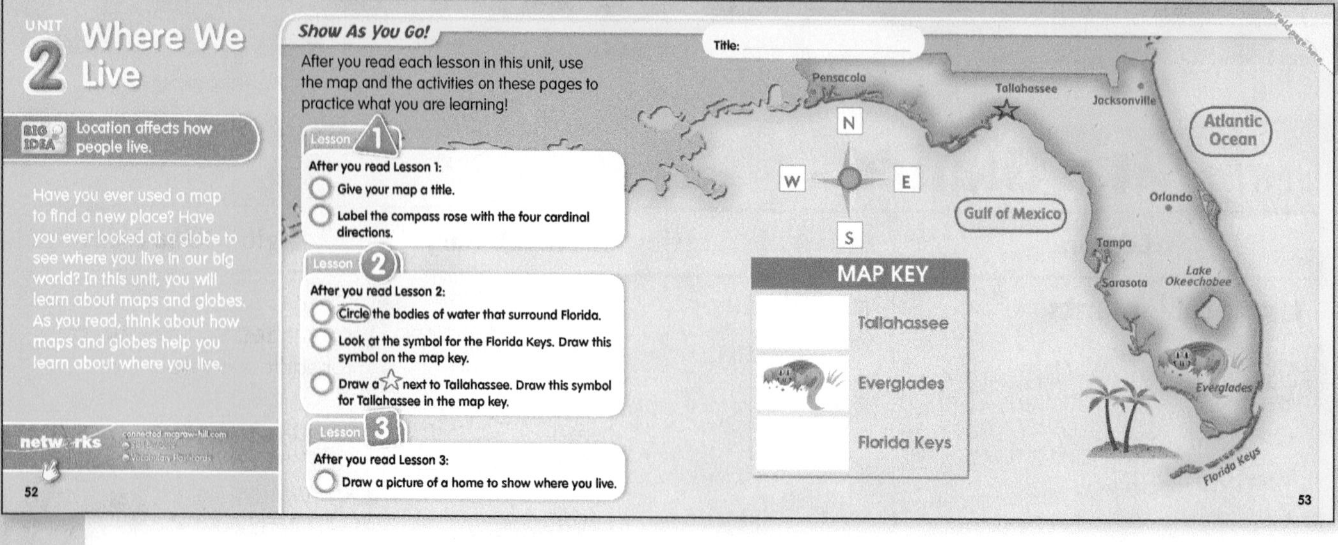
UNIT 2 Where We Live

BIG IDEA Location affects how people live.

Have you ever used a map to find a new place? Have you ever looked at a globe to see where you live in our big world? In this unit, you will learn about maps and globes. As you read, think about how maps and globes help you learn about where you live.

networks

52

Show As You Go!

After you read each lesson in this unit, use the map and the activities on these pages to practice what you are learning!

Lesson 1

After you read Lesson 1:
- Give your map a title.
- Label the compass rose with the four cardinal directions.

Lesson 2

After you read Lesson 2:
- Circle the bodies of water that surround Florida.
- Look at the symbol for the Florida Keys. Draw this symbol on the map key.
- Draw a ☆ next to Tallahassee. Draw this symbol for Tallahassee in the map key.

Lesson 3

After you read Lesson 3:
- Draw a picture of a home to show where you live.

Title:
Pensacola
Tallahassee
Jacksonville
Atlantic Ocean
N
W
E
S
Gulf of Mexico
MAP KEY
Tallahassee
Everglades
Florida Keys
Orlando
Tampa
Sarasota
Lake Okeechobee
Everglades
Florida Keys

53

Introduce the Unit

Diagnostic Assessment

Read aloud the statements below. Ask students to indicate how much they know about each topic by holding up fingers using the following scale:

1 = I know very little about this.
2 = I know something about this.
3 = I know a lot about this.

- I know about maps and globes.
- I know about physical maps and political maps.
- I know about cities.
- I know about the landforms.
- I know about the Atlantic Ocean.
- I know about the Gulf of Mexico.
- I know about location and physical environment.
- I know about the weather.

Say: *In this unit, we will learn about maps and globes. We will also read about how location, or where we live, affects our lives.*

Active Teaching

BIG IDEA **Location affects how people live.** In this geography unit, students will learn that location affects how people live. Students will use the ***Show As You Go!*** pages throughout their study of this unit. Students will use information from the lesson to complete the activities.

At this point, have students fold back the top corner of page 53. This will help them flip back to this page as needed. Explain to students that at the end of the unit, they will use the information collected on these pages to complete their Big Idea Project.

Differentiated Instruction

Approaching Review the directions with students and help them define any unfamiliar words. After each lesson, allow students to work in pairs to complete the activity.

Beyond Pair students with an approaching-level or ELL student. Have beyond-level students read the directions and help define unfamiliar words.

ELL Have students circle key words in the directions. Define unfamiliar words. After students complete the lessons, have them work with a partner to discuss and record information on these pages.

Common Core Standards
R.I.6: Distinguish between information provided by pictures or other illustrations and information provided by the words in a text. R.I.7: Use the illustrations and details in a text to describe its key ideas.

Use Visuals and Text

A visual can be a drawing, a picture, or a map. Visuals often give clues about the text. Text is something that is written. As you read, look at the visuals to help you understand the key ideas, or important information in the text.

Visuals help you understand what you will read.

54

 **Learn It**

To help you use visuals and text:

1. Before you read the text, look at the visuals. What do they show?
2. As you read the text, look for key ideas.
3. After you read, think about how the visuals and text help you understand the key ideas.

Take out your bug spray and get ready for the swamps of southern United States! These swamps are near the Gulf Coast in Louisiana. Swamps are one kind of wetland. That means they are wet most, or all, of the year. A swamp is low land that is covered with water and plants.

The text gives key ideas.

 **Try It**

What did you learn from the visual and text on page 54? Write down the key ideas below.

Key Ideas in Visuals

- trees
- grass
- water

Key Ideas in Text

- These swamps are located in Louisiana
- A wetland is land that is wet most, or all, of the year.
- A swamp is low land that is covered with water and plants.

 **Apply It**

Read the text below and look at the picture. Underline key ideas.

Swamps are home to many kinds of animals. You would see everything from snakes and lizards to birds and fish. Of course, you can't forget about the alligators!

55

Common Core Standards **R.I.6** Distinguish between information provided by pictures or other illustrations and information provided by the words in a text. **R.I.7** Use the illustrations and details in a text to describe its key ideas.

Reading Skill

Active Teaching

LEARN IT Use Visuals and Text

Read the LEARN IT activity together. Share this active reading strategy to help students use visuals and text.

Say: *Before I read, I look at the visuals, or pictures. The visuals give me clues about what I will read. Then as I read, I think about how the visuals and the text help me understand the key ideas.*

TRY IT Encourage students to try the modeled strategy as they complete the TRY IT activity.

APPLY IT Have students complete the APPLY IT activity.

Ask:

1. *What are examples of visuals?* (pictures, drawings, or maps) **L1**
2. *What can you do before reading the text?* (look at the visuals) **L2**
3. *How do visuals help you understand the text?* (Visuals give clues about the text.) **L3**

Differentiated Instruction

▶ **Approaching** Review the LEARN IT activity as a small group. Do the TRY IT activity together. Have students complete the APPLY IT activity independently. Regroup to compare and correct students' answers.

▶ **Beyond** Provide one or two additional examples. Have students list the key details from the text and visuals on the graphic organizer.

▶ **ELL** Point to and define the words *visuals* and *text*. Model the strategy slowly with students using the LEARN IT activity. Then have volunteers repeat the strategy. Do the TRY IT activity together. Have students work in pairs to complete the APPLY IT activity. Regroup to compare and correct students' answers.

networks

Go to connected.mcgraw-hill.com for additional resources:

- Skill Builders
- Graphic Organizers

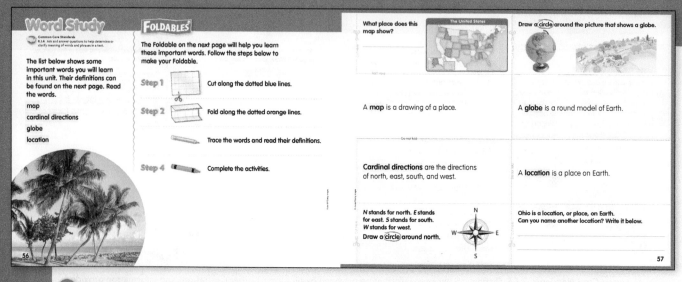

Words to Know

Active Teaching

FOLDABLES

1. Go to connected.mcgraw-hill.com for flashcards to introduce the unit vocabulary to students.

2. Read the words on the list on page 56 and have students repeat them after you.

3. Guide students as they complete steps 1 through 4 of the Foldable.

4. Have students use the Foldable to practice the vocabulary words independently or with a partner.

networks

Go to connected.mcgraw-hill.com for additional resources:
- Vocabulary Flashcards
- Vocabulary Games
- Graphic Organizers

GO Vocabulary!

Use the graphic organizer below to help students practice the meanings of the words from the list. Model for students how to complete the graphic organizer using the word *cardinal directions*. Have students complete the graphic organizer for the other words independently or with a partner.

WORD	VISUAL
cardinal directions	N W ← → E S
DEFINITION the directions of north, south, east, and west	**PERSONAL ASSOCIATION** I can use cardinal directions to find places.

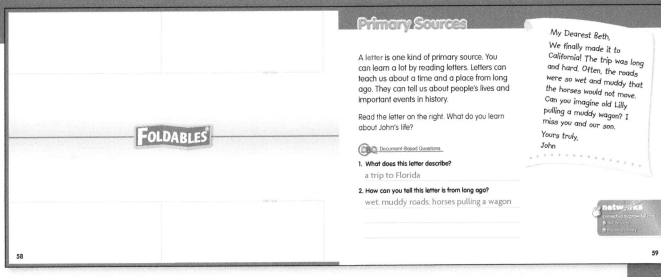

Primary Sources

A letter is one kind of primary source. You can learn a lot by reading letters. Letters can teach us about a time and a place from long ago. They can tell us about people's lives and important events in history.

Read the letter on the right. What do you learn about John's life?

DBQ Document-Based Questions

1. **What does this letter describe?**
   a trip to Florida

2. **How can you tell this letter is from long ago?**
   wet, muddy roads; horses pulling a wagon

My Dearest Beth,

We finally made it to California! The trip was long and hard. Often, the roads were so wet and muddy that the horses would not move. Can you imagine old Lilly pulling a muddy wagon? I miss you and our son.

Yours truly,
John

Common Core Standards **RI.4** Ask and answer questions to help determine or clarify the meaning of words and phrases in a text.

Primary Sources

Differentiated Instruction

 ELL Help students make connections to the vocabulary words in their own languages. Say each word and show a picture. Then have students repeat after you. Ask students to translate the word in their own language. For example, below is a Spanish translation of the vocabulary words in the Foldable.

map–mapa

globe–globo

cardinal directions–puntos cardinales

location–lugar

WORD PLAY

Play a guessing game to help students practice the vocabulary. Before you begin, write the words on the board. Provide one clue at a time, from the most challenging clue to the easiest, until students can guess the word. For example, you can use these clues with the word *globe*:

- I am a model of Earth.
- I show all land and water.
- You can spin me to find a location, or place.
- I am round.

Add additional words from the unit to make the game more interesting and challenging.

Active Teaching

Use page 59 to teach students that a letter is one type of primary source. Explain that letters can be used to learn more about people, places, and events from the past. If possible, provide copies of letters written by famous people. You can obtain copies through the Library of Congress, or you can do an online image search for letters.

Ask: *What can we learn about life in the past from letters we read?*

netw**o**rks

Go to connected.mcgraw-hill.com for additional resources:

- Skill Builders
- Resource Library

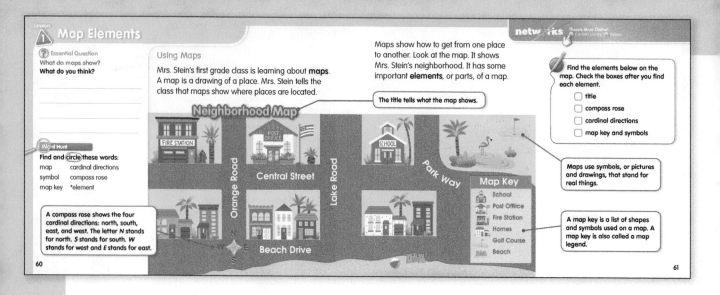

Activate Prior Knowledge

Divide the class into pairs or small groups for a Think-Pair-Share activity. Pass out various maps for students to explore, including:

- city, state, or country maps
- theme park maps
- zoo maps
- museum maps
- historical maps

Ask students to discuss the characteristics of the maps. Then have a whole-class discussion about the uses and elements of the various maps.

Say: *In this lesson, we are going to learn about the elements, or parts, of maps.*

? **Essential Question** **What do maps show?**

Have students explain what they understand about the Essential Question. Discuss their responses. Explain that everything they learn in this lesson will help them understand the Essential Question better. Remind them to think about how the Essential Question connects to the unit Big Idea: Location affects how people live.

networks

Go to connected.mcgraw-hill.com for additional resources:

- Interactive Whiteboard Lessons
- Worksheets
- Assessment
- Content Library

Active Teaching

Words To Know Have students look through the lesson to find the words that are listed in the Word Hunt. Have them read the definitions of the content vocabulary words. Point out the academic vocabulary word *element*.

Say: *When we examine something, we look at its elements, or parts.*

Go over the elements, or parts, of a book with students (for example, the title page, Table of Contents, glossary, and index).

Ask: *What other things have elements, or parts, that we can examine? (a Web site, a magazine, nutrition information, a model airplane, and so forth).*

Develop Comprehension

Read pages 60–61 together. Point to the elements of the map, making sure that students understand each part.

Ask:

1. *What are the elements of a map?* **L1**
2. *What are cardinal directions?* **L1**
3. *Why are maps important?* (Maps show where places are located and how to get from one place to another.) **L3**

Differentiated Instruction

▶ **ELL** Read the selection together and have students echo-read. Go over key terms, such as *map key, symbol, cardinal directions, compass rose,* and *title*. Give students post-it notes and have them identify each element on a map on the wall.

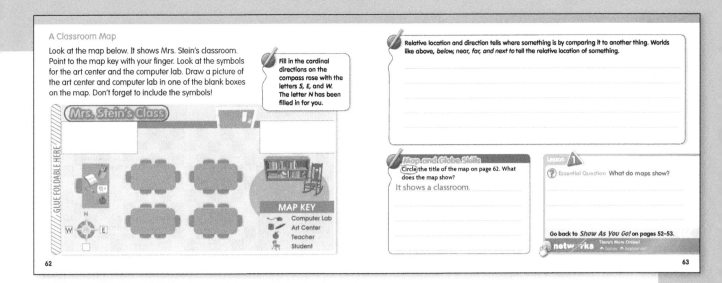

A Classroom Map

Look at the map below. It shows Mrs. Stein's classroom. Point to the map key with your finger. Look at the symbols for the art center and the computer lab. Draw a picture of the art center and computer lab in one of the blank boxes on the map. Don't forget to include the symbols!

> Fill in the cardinal directions on the compass rose with the letters *S*, *E*, and *W*. The letter *N* has been filled in for you.

Mrs. Stein's Class

GLUE FOLDABLE HERE

MAP KEY
- Computer Lab
- Art Center
- Teacher
- Student

62

> Relative location and direction tells where something is by comparing it to another thing. Worlds like above, *below*, near, *far*, and *next to* tell the relative location of something.

Map and Globe Skills
Circle the title of the map on page 62. What does the map show?
It shows a classroom.

Lesson 1
(?) Essential Question What do maps show?

Go back to *Show As You Go!* on pages 52–53.

networks There's More Online!

63

Active Teaching

Remind students that they have already read about map symbols.

Ask: *What are some symbols that can stand for the computer lab? What symbol can we use for the art center?* (a computer screen or mouse for the computer lab and a paint brush for the art center)

Guide students as they complete the activities on pages 62–63. Discuss their responses.

Develop Comprehension

Ask:

1. *What does the word* symbol *mean?* **L1**

2. *What symbols does the map key on page 62 show?* **L2**

3. *How is a map key helpful?* (Map keys help us identify, or find, places on a map.) **L3**

Before summarizing the lesson, give students additional practice using map elements. Use the Foldable instructions under Page Power in the next column to guide students.

Summarize the lesson. Then have students respond to the Essential Question. Discuss their responses. Have students revisit their response on page 60 and compare it to their response at the end of the lesson. Discuss how their answers have changed.

> ***Show As You Go!*** Remind students to go back to the Unit Opener and complete the activities for this lesson.

Page Power

FOLDABLES Interact more with the page. Have students create a Notebook Foldable to assist them in developing their understanding of maps and map elements.

1. Provide students with a copy of Foldable 2A from the Notebook Foldables section at the back of this book.

2. Have students cut out the Foldable and glue its anchor tab where indicated on page 62.

3. On the Foldable flap, have students draw two lines (one horizontal, one vertical) to create four squares. Ask students to write one of the following words in each square: *title, map key, symbol,* and *cardinal directions.*

4. Ask students to write a definition or draw a picture for each word, using the map elements on page 62.

Response to Intervention

(?) Essential Question **What do maps show?**

If . . . students cannot answer the Essential Question, "What do maps show?"

. . . .

Then . . . take students back to pages 60 and 61. Point out the map elements and go over their definitions.

Ask: *What are the elements of a map?*

Using a marker or chalk, draw a simple map on the board. Then, have students go up to the board and label the map elements. Following the discussion, allow students to respond to the Essential Question again.

Unit 2 • Lesson 1   **62–63**

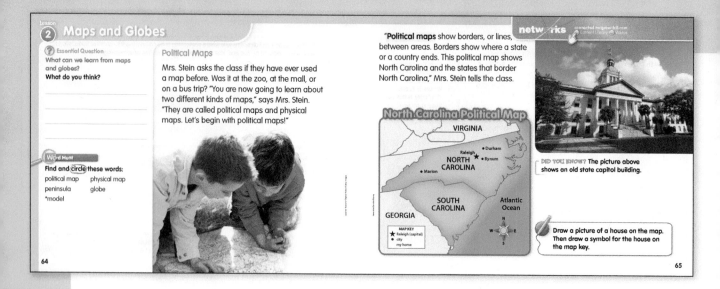

Essential Question
What can we learn from maps and globes?
What do you think?

_____
_____
_____
_____

Word Hunt
Find and circle these words:
political map   physical map
peninsula   globe
*model

Political Maps

Mrs. Stein asks the class if they have ever used a map before. Was it at the zoo, at the mall, or on a bus trip? "You are now going to learn about two different kinds of maps," says Mrs. Stein. "They are called political maps and physical maps. Let's begin with political maps!"

"**Political maps** show borders, or lines, between areas. Borders show where a state or a country ends. This political map shows North Carolina and the states that border North Carolina," Mrs. Stein tells the class.

North Carolina Political Map

VIRGINIA
NORTH CAROLINA
Raleigh ★ • Durham
• Bynum
• Marion
SOUTH CAROLINA
Atlantic Ocean
GEORGIA

MAP KEY
★ Raleigh (capital)
• city
my home

N W E S

DID YOU KNOW? The picture above shows an old state capitol building.

Draw a picture of a house on the map. Then draw a symbol for the house on the map key.

64

65

Lesson 2

Activate Prior Knowledge

To help motivate students and assess their understanding of maps and globes, gather students into circles (keeping each circle limited to five or six students). Follow these steps for a quick geography game:

- Toss an inflatable globe to each student. (You can also use a state map, the United States, or a world map and have students pass it along in a circle.)
- Ask them to close their eyes and point to a location.
- Then ask them to determine whether the location is land or water.

To expose students to places around the world, say the name of the place they have identified.

Say: *In this lesson, we are going to learn how to use maps and globes.*

Essential Question **What can we learn from maps and globes?**

Have students explain what they understand about the Essential Question. Discuss their responses. Explain that everything they learn in this lesson will help them understand the Essential Question better. Remind them to think about how the Essential Question connects to the unit Big Idea: Location affects how people live.

Active Teaching

Words To Know Have students look through the lesson to find the vocabulary words in the Word Hunt. Have them read the definitions of the content vocabulary words.

Define the academic vocabulary word *model* (a small copy of something). Show students a globe. Explain that the globe is a model of Earth. If possible, provide examples of other models, such as a model airplane, train, or car.

Ask: *Can you think of other models you have seen?*

Develop Comprehension

Have students preview the selection, pointing out visuals, titles, and heads in this lesson. Then read pages 64–65 together. Guide students through the written activities. Discuss their responses.

Ask:

1. *What is a political map?* (A political map shows borders, or lines, between places.) **L1**
2. *Which states border your state?* **L2**
3. *Which city is closest to where you live?* **L2**

Differentiated Instruction

▶ **ELL** Have students look at the map on page 65. Explain that this map is called a political map. Have students run their fingers along the border. Explain that political maps use borders, or lines, to show where a state or country ends. Provide other maps and have students trace borders of other states or countries with their fingers.

Now the class looks at a **physical map**. Mrs. Stein explains that physical maps show different kinds of land, such as peninsulas and swamps. Physical maps also show bodies of water, such as oceans, lakes, rivers, and gulfs. Look at the physical map. Do you live near any of the places on this map?

DID YOU KNOW?
Utah is home to The Bonneville Salt Flats. The smooth salt surface is ideal for auto and motorcycle racing.

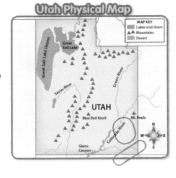

Utah Physical Map

MAP KEY
Lakes and rivers
Mountains
Desert

Great Salt Lake Desert

Great Salt Lake

Sevier River

Green River

UTAH
Blue Bell Knoll

Mt. Peale

Glenn Canyon

Colorado River

1. Follow the Colorado River with your pencil.
2. Draw a circle around the Salt Lake Desert.

66

Look at the pictures on the right. They show a place on the map. Write the letter for each place in the correct box on the map below.

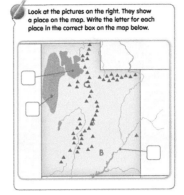

A. Great Salt Lake

B. Great Salt Lake Desert

C. Canyon along the Green River

67

Active Teaching

Have students look at the physical map. Explain that a physical map shows different kinds of land and water. Point to landmarks and water on the map.

Read and discuss pages 66–67 together. Guide students through the activities. Discuss their responses.

Develop Comprehension

Ask:

1. *What are the names of the rivers on the map?* **L2**

2. *Which bodies of water are in this state?* **L2**

3. *How are physical and political maps the same? How are they different?* (Same: physical and political maps both show places. Different: physical maps show land and water; political maps show borders, or lines, between places) **L3**

✔ Formative Assessment

Have students write three facts they have learned about political and physical maps. For example, for political maps students might report:

• Political maps show borders, or lines, between places.

Use this assessment to monitor students' understanding and to identify need for intervention.

Differentiated Instruction

▶ **Approaching** Have partners read the selection together. Then have them complete the following sentence frames:

I live in the state of _____.
I live in the city of _____.

▶ **Beyond** Have students work in pairs. Ask them to compare and contrast physical and political maps using a Venn diagram.

▶ **ELL** Write the terms "Political Map" and "Physical Map" on the board. Say these terms aloud and have students repeat after you. Read pages 64–67 together. Stop after each paragraph and ask students for key details that go under each term. Write the details under the corresponding term.

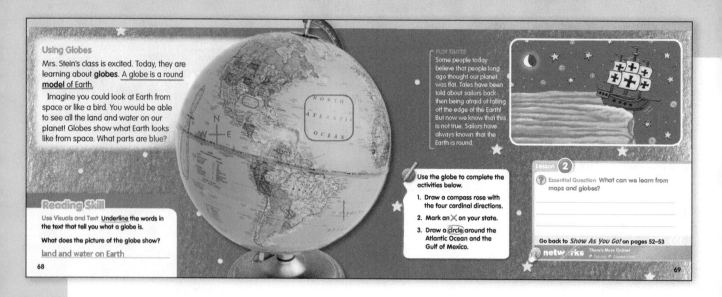

Using Globes

Mrs. Stein's class is excited. Today, they are learning about **globes**. A globe is a round **model** of Earth.

Imagine you could look at Earth from space or like a bird. You would be able to see all the land and water on our planet! Globes show what Earth looks like from space. What parts are blue?

FUN FACTS
Some people today believe that people long ago thought our planet was flat. Tales have been told about sailors back then being afraid of falling off the edge of the Earth! But now we know that this is not true. Sailors have always known that the Earth is round.

Reading Skill

Use Visuals and Text <u>Underline</u> the words in the text that tell you what a globe is.

What does the picture of the globe show?

land and water on Earth

Use the globe to complete the activities below.

1. Draw a compass rose with the four cardinal directions.
2. Mark an ✕ on your state.
3. Draw a circle around the Atlantic Ocean and the Gulf of Mexico.

Lesson 2

❓ **Essential Question** What can we learn from maps and globes?

Go back to *Show As You Go!* on pages 52–53

networks There's More Online!

Lesson 2

Active Teaching

If possible, provide a real globe for students to explore. Have them locate the United States. Then have them find their state, the Atlantic Ocean, and the Gulf of Mexico. Explain that globes also include elements like a compass rose with cardinal directions and a map key with symbols. Have students locate these on the globe.

Develop Comprehension

Read pages 68–69 together. Guide students through the written activities. Discuss students' responses.

Ask:

1. *What is a globe?* **L1**
2. *What bodies of water does the globe show?* **L1**
3. *How is a globe different from a map?* (A globe is a round model of Earth. A map is a flat drawing of a place.) **L3**

Summarize the lesson with the class. Then have students respond to the Essential Question. Discuss their responses. Have students revisit their response on page 64 and compare it to their response at the end of the lesson. Discuss how their answers changed.

Show As You Go! Remind students to go back to the Unit Opener and complete the activities for this lesson.

Response to Intervention

❓ **Essential Question** **What can we learn from maps and globes?**

If . . . students cannot give a substantiated response to the Essential Question, "What can we learn from maps and globes?"

....

Then . . . display a physical map of their state and a globe. Discuss the features of maps and globes. Have students point to the land and water on each. Then have students locate cities, landforms, and bodies of water on the physical map. Have students locate the Atlantic Ocean and the Gulf of Mexico on the globe. Following the discussion, have students respond to the Essential Question again.

networks

Go to **connected.mcgraw-hill.com** for additional resources:
- Interactive Whiteboard Lessons
- Worksheets
- Assessment
- Skill Builders

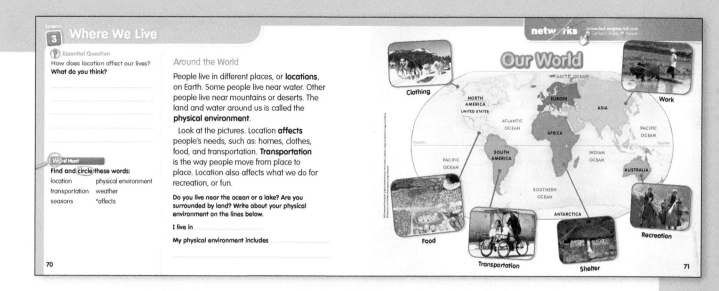

Lesson 3 — Where We Live

Essential Question
How does location affect our lives?
What do you think?

Word Hunt
Find and circle these words:
- location
- transportation
- seasons
- physical environment
- weather
- *affects

Around the World

People live in different places, or **locations**, on Earth. Some people live near water. Other people live near mountains or deserts. The land and water around us is called the **physical environment**.

Look at the pictures. Location **affects** people's needs, such as: homes, clothes, food, and transportation. **Transportation** is the way people move from place to place. Location also affects what we do for recreation, or fun.

Do you live near the ocean or a lake? Are you surrounded by land? Write about your physical environment on the lines below.

I live in

My physical environment includes

Our World

Clothing · Work · Food · Transportation · Shelter · Recreation

(Map labels: ARCTIC OCEAN, NORTH AMERICA, UNITED STATES, ATLANTIC OCEAN, EUROPE, ASIA, PACIFIC OCEAN, AFRICA, SOUTH AMERICA, INDIAN OCEAN, PACIFIC OCEAN, AUSTRALIA, SOUTHERN OCEAN, ANTARCTICA, Equator)

70 / 71

Lesson 3

Activate Prior Knowledge

Tell students that you are going to name a place (for example, the beach, mountains, the North Pole). Have them close their eyes and imagine they are in this place. Ask volunteers to tell you what they see.

Ask:
- What do you see around you?
- What is the weather like?
- How are you dressed?
- What can you do for fun in this place?
- What kinds of food would you eat here?

Say: In this lesson, we are going to learn about how location, or where we live, affects our lives.

Essential Question How does location affect our lives?

Have students explain what they understand about the Essential Question. Discuss their responses. Explain that everything they learn in this lesson will help them understand the Essential Question better. Remind them to think about how the Essential Question connects to the unit Big Idea: Location affects how people live.

Active Teaching

Words To Know Have students look through the lesson to find the words that are listed in the Word Hunt. Have them read the definitions of the content vocabulary words. Point out the academic vocabulary word *affects*.

Say: The word affects means to make something happen. Let's think about how something affects us. How does rain affect us?

Write students' responses on the board. If necessary, use other examples of things that might affect students (for example, missing the bus to school).

Develop Comprehension

Ask students to look at the pictures and map on page 71. Explain that the pictures show how people live in different locations, or places, on Earth. Read page 70 aloud with students. Guide students as they complete the activity.

Ask:

1. What is another word for location? **L1**

2. What do the pictures show? (They show how location affects people's lives around the world.) **L2**

3. What things does location affect? **L2**

Differentiated Instruction

▶ **ELL** Explain to students that visuals, or pictures, help readers understand what they are reading. Have volunteers describe what is happening in the pictures. Then ask students to write which of the following the pictures are showing: clothes, food, transportation, recreation, or homes. Tell students that some pictures may show more than one of the categories.

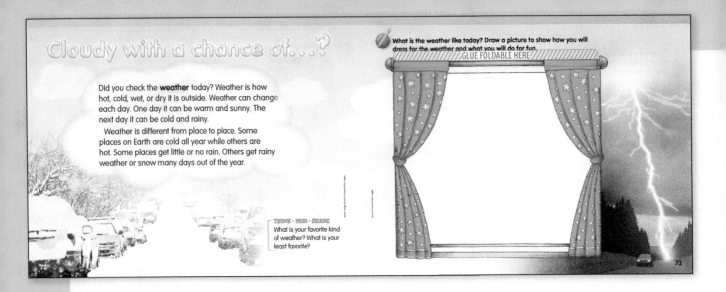

Cloudy with a chance of...?

Did you check the **weather** today? Weather is how hot, cold, wet, or dry it is outside. Weather can change each day. One day it can be warm and sunny. The next day it can be cold and rainy.

Weather is different from place to place. Some places on Earth are cold all year while others are hot. Some places get little or no rain. Others get rainy weather or snow many days out of the year.

THINK · PAIR · SHARE
What is your favorite kind of weather? What is your least favorite?

What is the weather like today? Draw a picture to show how you will dress for the weather and what you will do for fun.
GLUE FOLDABLE HERE

72 / 73

Lesson 3

Active Teaching

Point out the pictures on pages 72–73.

Ask: *What do the pictures show? Have you ever seen snow or visited a cold place?*

Tell students that weather is different from place to place. Read page 72 with students. Guide students as they complete the activities on pages 72–73.

Develop Comprehension

Ask:

1. *What is weather?* **L1**
2. *Describe the weather where you live.* **L1**
3. *How would you dress for cold, snowy weather?* **L2**

Page Power

FOLDABLES Interact more with the page. Have students create a Notebook Foldable to assist them in developing their understanding of how weather affects people's daily lives.

1. Provide each student with Foldable 2B from the Notebook Foldables section at the back of this book.

2. Have students cut out the Foldable and glue its anchor tab where indicated on page 73.

3. On the Foldable flap, have students complete the following sentence frames for a weather story:

    Today, the weather is _____.

    I will wear _____.

    For fun, I will _____.

4. On the other side of the Foldable, have students predict what the weather will be like tomorrow.

✔ Formative Assessment

Have students respond to the true and false statements below. Use this assessment to monitor student understanding and identify need for intervention.

- Weather is how hot, cold, wet, or dry it is outside.
- Weather is not different from place to place.
- Weather can change each day.
- Weather does not affect how we dress and what we do for fun.

As an optional assesment, have students write a letter or send an ePal letter to a friend in another part of the country. Explain that in their letter, they should describe where they live, including their physical surroundings, weather, and what they can do for fun.

Clarifying Misconceptions

Some students may not understand that the weather can be different in different parts of the country or world. To help students understand this concept, bring in a weather map from your local newspaper. Have students create a chart showing temperatures from major cities across the United States.

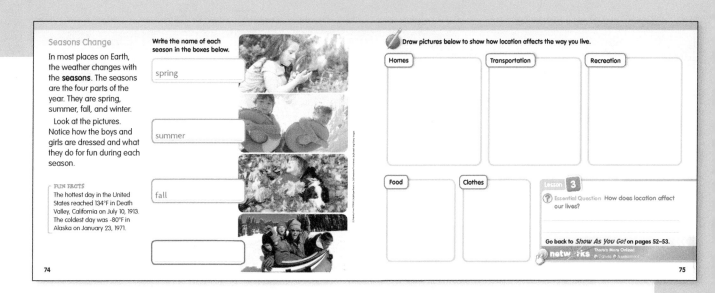

Seasons Change

In most places on Earth, the weather changes with the **seasons**. The seasons are the four parts of the year. They are spring, summer, fall, and winter.

Look at the pictures. Notice how the boys and girls are dressed and what they do for fun during each season.

FUN FACTS
The hottest day in the United States reached 134°F in Death Valley, California on July 10, 1913. The coldest day was -80°F in Alaska on January 23, 1971.

Write the name of each season in the boxes below.

spring

summer

fall

Draw pictures below to show how location affects the way you live.

Homes

Transportation

Recreation

Food

Clothes

Lesson 3

Essential Question How does location affect our lives?

Go back to *Show As You Go!* on pages 52–53.

networks There's More Online!

Active Teaching

Before students read page 74 and complete the activities, hold a classroom discussion about the weather and seasons.

Say: *In the Southeast, the weather is warm and mild most of the year. But as we just read on page 72, many places around the world get snow and freezing temperatures in the winter. The winters in the Southeast are mild. Snow and freezing temperatures are rare.*

Ask: *What do you know about the four seasons?*

Guide students through the activities on pages 74–75. Discuss students' responses.

Develop Comprehension
Ask:

1. *What are the four seasons?* **L1**

2. *How would your life be different if you lived in another part of the world?* **L3**

Summarize the lesson with the class. Then have students respond to the Essential Question. Discuss their responses. Have students revisit their response on page 70 and compare it to their response at the end of the lesson. Discuss how their answers changed.

Use the leveled reader, *On Top of the World*, to extend and enrich students' understanding of how people's lives are affected in Barrow, Alaska. A lesson plan for this leveled reader can be found on pages T24–T25 at the front of this Teacher Edition.

Show As You Go! Remind students to go back to complete the activities on the Unit Opener.

Response to Intervention

(?) Essential Question **How does location affect our lives?**

If . . . students cannot give a substantiated response to the Essential Question, "How does location affect our lives?"

. . . .

Then . . . Have students re-read pages 70–74. Compare their drawings on page 75 with the images on the map on page 71. Have students explain how location might affect people. Following the discussion, allow students to respond to the Essential Question again.

networks

Go to connected.mcgraw-hill.com for additional resources:
- Interactive Whiteboard Lessons
- Skill Builders
- Videos
- Assessment
- Content Library

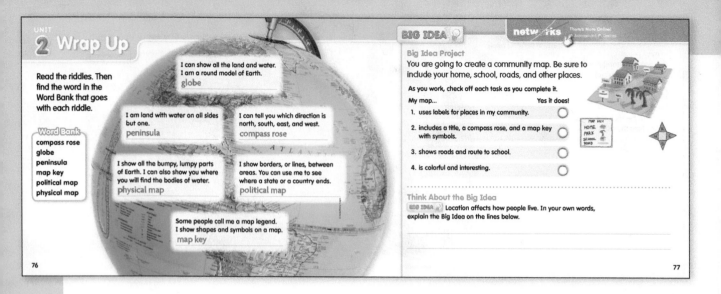

Read the riddles. Then find the word in the Word Bank that goes with each riddle.

Word Bank
- compass rose
- globe
- peninsula
- map key
- political map
- physical map

I can show all the land and water. I am a round model of Earth.
globe

I am land with water on all sides but one.
peninsula

I can tell you which direction is north, south, east, and west.
compass rose

I show all the bumpy, lumpy parts of Earth. I can also show you where you will find the bodies of water.
physical map

I show borders, or lines, between areas. You can use me to see where a state or a country ends.
political map

Some people call me a map legend. I show shapes and symbols on a map.
map key

BIG IDEA

Big Idea Project

You are going to create a community map. Be sure to include your home, school, roads, and other places.

As you work, check off each task as you complete it.

My map...   Yes it does!

1. uses labels for places in my community.   ○
2. includes a title, a compass rose, and a map key with symbols. ○
3. shows roads and route to school.   ○
4. is colorful and interesting.   ○

Think About the Big Idea

BIG IDEA Location affects how people live. In your own words, explain the Big Idea on the lines below.

76   77

Unit 2 Wrap Up

Word Riddles

Have students complete the activity on page 76 to review the Unit vocabulary. Encourage students to read the riddles at least two times before writing their answers. If necessary, walk them through the first example.

BIG IDEA Unit Project

Students will be making a map to show what they learned in Unit 2.

1. Read the checklist together and answer any questions students may have about the project.
2. Help students brainstorm ideas for their maps, including materials they will need.
3. If possible, send a letter home to parents explaining the unit project and requesting any materials students will need.
4. Display students' maps in the classroom. Have each students give a brief presentation about their maps.
5. After students complete their projects, encourage self-reflection by asking
   - *What did you learn about community maps?*
   - *What changes would you make to your project if you did it again?*
6. To asses the project, refer to the rubric on the following page.

Differentiated Instruction

▶ **Approaching** Review the community map and map elements on pages 60 and 61 with students. If possible, create a sample community map that students can use as a model. Go over the checklist items on page 77 and answer any questions students may have.

▶ **Beyond** Have students write a short paragraph about their maps, including the types of materials they used.

▶ **ELL** Use the approaching level suggestions and allow students to work with a partner as they create their community maps.

Response To Intervention

BIG IDEA Location affects how people live.

If . . . students cannot give a substantiated response to the Big Idea, "Location affects how people live,"

. . . .

Then . . . write the words *food, clothing, shelter, transportation,* and *recreation.* Ask students to think about how location affects people in each of these categories. Following the discussion, allow students to respond to the Big Idea again.

networks

Go to **connected.mcgraw-hill.com** for additional resources:
- Games
- Assessment
- Group Technology Projects

Name _____ Date _____

Map Gallery Rubric

4 Exemplary	3 Accomplished	2 Developing	1 Beginning
The map:	**The map:**	**The map:**	**The map:**
☐ accurately portrays a community map that shows the student's home and school; also shows roads, including route to school.	☐ portrays a community map that shows the student's home and school; also shows roads, including route to school.	☐ attempts to portray a community map with some places in the community and some roads; may show route to school.	☐ may resemble a community map; may include student's home or school and some roads and route to school.
☐ includes labels with legible copy in neat handwriting; has no errors.	☐ includes labels with mostly legible copy in neat handwriting; has few errors.	☐ includes some labels with legible copy, showing some erasures; introduces some errors.	☐ includes some labels with illegible copy and many visible erasures; has many visible errors.
☐ includes the following map elements: a title, compass rose, and map key with accurate symbols.	☐ includes most of the following map elements: a title, compass rose, and map key with symbols.	☐ includes some of the following map elements: a title, compass rose, and map key with some symbols.	☐ may include the following map elements: a title, compass rose, and map key with some symbols.
☐ uses appropriate color, shape, texture, space, and value and demonstrates artistic interpretation.	☐ attempst to use appropriate color, shape, texture, space, and value with artistic interpretation.	☐ attempts to use appropriate color, shape, texture, space, and value with some artistic interpretation.	☐ does not use appropriate color, shape, texture, space, or value and has no artistic interpretation.

Grading Comments: _____

_____

_____

_____

_____

_____

_____

_____

_____

Project Score: _____

UNIT 3 Planner BEGINNING ECONOMICS

 **BIG IDEA** **Economics affects choices.**

Student Portfolio

- **Show As You Go!**
  Use these pages to introduce the Big Idea. Students record information specific to each lesson. They use these pages to help them plan their Big Idea Project.

netw**o**rks

- **Group Technology Project**
  Students use 21st century skills to complete a group extension activity of the unit project. Lesson plans, worksheets, and rubrics are available online.

Student Portfolio

- **Big Idea Project**
  Students will make a poster ad for a new good to be sold in a classroom store. The Big Idea Project rubric is on page 105W.

Buy a new box of crayons for just $2.00!

Reading Skills

Student Portfolio

- **Reading Skill: Main Topic and Details**
  Pages 80–81. Common Core State Standards RI.2

netw**o**rks

- **Skill Builders**
  Introduce and practice the reading skill.

Leveled Readers

Use the leveled reader *Jobs at School* (lesson plan on pages T26–T27) with Lesson 1 and *The Apple Man: The Story of John Chapman* (lesson plan on pages T28–T29) with Lesson 3.

Treasures Connection

Teach this unit with Treasures Unit 2, *From Wheat to Bread*, pages 62–67.

Social Studies Skills

Student Portfolio

- **Primary Sources: Pictures**
  Page 85

netw**o**rks

- **Skill Builders**
  Introduce and teach analyzing primary sources.

Activity Cards

- **Center for Social Studies Skills Investigation**
  Use the center activity cards to help students explore Primary Sources, Geography, and Citizenship.

FOLDABLES®

Student Portfolio

- Students can create vocabulary Foldables right in their portfolios.
- Additional Foldables templates can be found on pages R1–R8 of your Teacher Edition.

Assessment Solutions

- **McGraw-Hill networks™**
  Safe online testing features multiple question types that are easy to use and editable!
- **Self-Check Quizzes**
- **Worksheets**

UNIT 3 **At a Glance**

Lesson	Essential Question	Vocabulary	Digital Resources
1 Goods and Services	Why are goods and services important?	goods services *provide	Go to connected.mcgraw-hill.com for additional resources: • Interactive Whiteboard Lessons
2 Barter and Money	Why do we need money?	barter money *exchange	• Worksheets • Assessment
3 Producers, Sellers, and Buyers	Why do we need producers, sellers, and buyers?	producers sellers buyers	• Lesson Plans • Content Library • Skill Builders
4 Making Choices	Why do we make choices?	character *honesty *courage *responsibility	• Videos • Use Standards Tracker on **networks** to track students' progress.

*denotes academic vocabulary

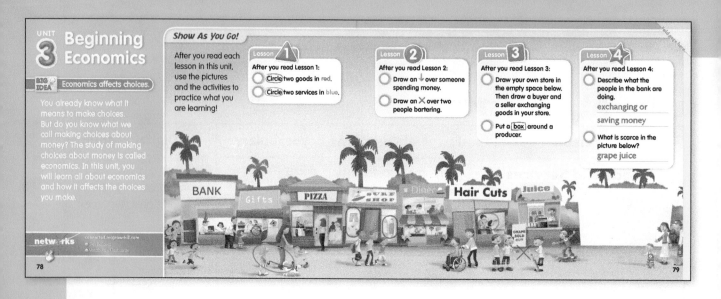

Introduce the Unit

☑ Diagnostic Assessment

Have students hold up a True or False card in response to these statements.

- All money is the same.
- You have to give up something when you spend your money.
- Goods and services are always available.
- People buy goods from sellers.
- Spending is more important that saving.
- We cannot have everything we want.

Active Teaching

BIG IDEA **Economics affects choices.**

In this unit about economics, students will learn that economics affects choices. Students will use the **Show As You Go!** pages throughout their study of this unit. They will use information from each lesson to complete the activities.

Explain to students that at the end of the unit, they will use the information collected on these pages to complete their Big Idea Project. At this point, have students fold back the corner of this page. This will help them flip back to this page as needed.

Differentiated Instruction

▶ **Approaching** Read the checklist items for students. Provide assistance to help students complete the checklist items after each lesson.

▶ **Beyond** Have students write captions for the pictures using vocabulary words from each lesson.

▶ **ELL** Read the checklist items with students. Say the key words in the checklist and have students repeat them after you. Paraphrase the directions, if necessary.

Common Core Standards
RI2: Identify the main topic and retell key details of a text.

Main Topic and Details

Every story that you read has a main topic. The main topic tells what the story is about. Every story also has details. Details give more information. Finding the main topic and details will help you understand what you read.

Learn It

To find the main topic and details:

1. Read the story below.
2. Decide what the story is about. This is the main topic.
3. Look for details. They tell you more about the main topic.

My family and I had fun on our trip to the planetarium. We saw big models of planets there. We even met a scientist! I bought a toy rocket to take home with me. I liked our trip to the planetarium.

← This is the main topic.

← This is a detail. Find two more details in the story and underline them.

Try It

Write the main topic and details from the story on page 80 in the chart below.

Main Topic

Detail → **Detail**

Apply It

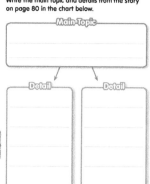

Read the story below. Circle the main topic. Underline the details.

On our trip we went to Myrtle Beach. We swam in the warm Atlantic Ocean. We made a big sand castle. We also went for a long walk and looked for seashells in the sand. I hope we go back to the beach soon!

Common Core Standard RI2: Identify the main topic and retell key details of a text.

Reading Skill

Active Teaching

LEARN IT Main Topic and Details

Read the first paragraph together. Share this active reading strategy for finding the main topic and key details:

Say: *As I read, I think, "What is this story about?" Answering this question helps me to find the main topic of the story. Once I know the main topic of the story, I pay attention to sentences that tell me more information about the main topic. Those sentences are the details.*

TRY IT
Encourage students to try the modeled strategy as they complete the TRY IT activity.

APPLY IT
After students have completed the APPLY IT activity,

Ask:

1. *What question should you ask yourself to help you find the main topic?* (What is this story about?) **L1**

2. *How can you tell which sentences in a story are the key details?* (They will tell you more about the main topic.) **L1**

3. *Why is it important to find the main topic and key details of a story?* (to help understand what you are reading) **L2**

Differentiated Instruction

▶ **Approaching** Review the LEARN IT activity as a small group. Do the TRY IT activity together. Have students complete the APPLY IT activity independently. Regroup to compare and correct.

▶ **Beyond** Have students write a short paragraph that includes a main topic and three key details. Have them exchange paragraphs with a partner. Each student should identify the main topic and key details of their partner's paragraph.

▶ **ELL** Reinforce the story words *family, trip, space center, rockets,* and *astronaut.* Read the story together. Provide assistance as students complete the activities on the pages. Model for students how to complete the graphic organizer.

networks

Go to connected.mcgraw-hill.com for additional resources:

- Skill Builders
- Graphic Organizers

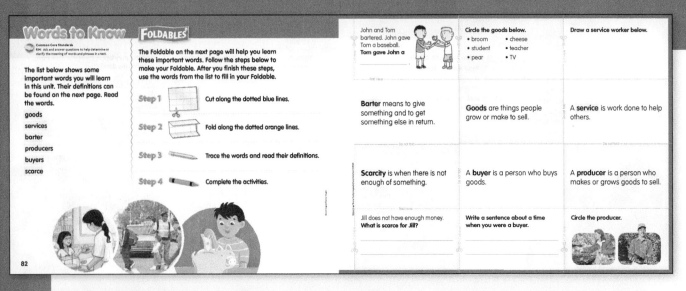

Words to Know — FOLDABLES

The list below shows some important words you will learn in this unit. Their definitions can be found on the next page. Read the words.

goods
services
barter
producers
buyers
scarce

The Foldable on the next page will help you learn these important words. Follow the steps below to make your Foldable. After you finish these steps, use the words from the list to fill in your Foldable.

Step 1 Cut along the dotted blue lines.

Step 2 Fold along the dotted orange lines.

Step 3 Trace the words and read their definitions.

Step 4 Complete the activities.

John and Tom bartered. John gave Tom a baseball. **Tom gave John a**

Circle the goods below.
- broom
- student
- pear
- cheese
- teacher
- TV

Draw a service worker below.

Barter means to give something and to get something else in return.

Goods are things people grow or make to sell.

A **service** is work done to help others.

Scarcity is when there is not enough of something.

A **buyer** is a person who buys goods.

A **producer** is a person who makes or grows goods to sell.

Jill does not have enough money. **What is scarce for Jill?**

Write a sentence about a time when you were a buyer.

Circle the producer.

🔵 **Common Core Standards RI4:** Ask and answer questions to help determine or clarify the meaning of words and phrases in a text.

Words to Know

Active Teaching

FOLDABLES

1. Go to connected.mcgraw-hill.com for flashcards to introduce the unit vocabulary to students.

2. Read the words on the list on page 82 and have students repeat them after you.

3. Guide students as they complete steps 1 through 4 of the Foldable.

4. Have students use the Foldable to practice the vocabulary words independently or with a partner.

networks

Go to connected.mcgraw-hill.com for additional resources:
- Graphic Organizers
- Vocabulary Flashcards
- Vocabulary Games

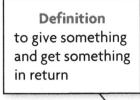

GO Vocabulary!

Use the graphic organizer below to help students practice the meanings of the words from the list. Model for students how to complete the graphic organizer using the word *barter*. Have students complete the graphic organizer for the other words independently or with a parter.

Definition to give something and get something in return	**Description** (in own words) to exchange one thing for another

Word
barter

Examples (from own life) • lunch items • toys	**Non-Examples** to give something away and get nothing in return

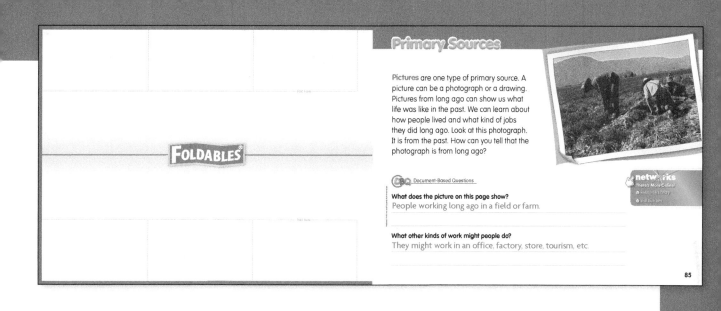

Pictures are one type of primary source. A picture can be a photograph or a drawing. Pictures from long ago can show us what life was like in the past. We can learn about how people lived and what kind of jobs they did long ago. Look at this photograph. It is from the past. How can you tell that the photograph is from long ago?

DBQ Document-Based Questions

What does the picture on this page show?
People working long ago in a field or farm.

What other kinds of work might people do?
They might work in an office, factory, store, tourism, etc.

netw⬤rks
There's More Online!
• Resource Library
• Skill Builders

85

Differentiated Instruction

▶ **ELL** Act out each word with students. For example, for the word *buyer*, act like you are buying something at a store. Point to yourself and say, *"I am a buyer when I buy things at the store."* Have students repeat the word *buyer*. Have students describe a time when they were buyers. Repeat the activity with the words *seller*, *producer*, *goods*, *services*, *scarcity*, *save*, *spend*, *opportunity cost*, and *save*.

W O R D   P L A Y

Guess My Word

Play Guess My Word to help students practice the vocabulary.

1. Write each word on a slip of paper, fold, and place in a hat or container.
2. Have each student choose a word from the hat or container and give clues to the meaning of the word.
3. The other students should guess the word.
4. Allow students to take turns giving verbal clues and guessing.

Active Teaching

Use page 85 to teach your students about using pictures to learn about people, places, and events. Read the page together. Discuss the photograph on page 85. Guide students through the written activities.

Ask: *How can pcitures help us understand what life was like long ago? How do photographs tell a story about people, places, and events?*

netw⬤rks

Go to connected.mcgraw-hill.com for additional resources:
• Skill Builders
• Resource Library

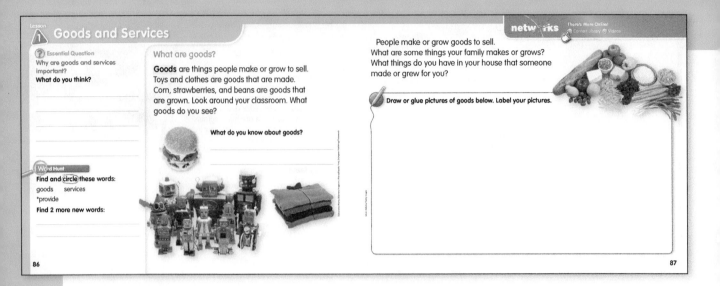

Lesson 1

Activate Prior Knowledge

Engage students in a discussion about goods.

Ask: *Who has heard of a good? Can someone give me a definition of a good? What goods do you see in our classroom?*

Explain that in this lesson, students will learn about the importance of goods and services.

(?) Essential Question Why are goods and services important?

Have students explain what they understand about the Essential Question. Discuss their responses. Explain that everything they learn in this lesson will help them understand the Essential Question better. Remind them to think about how the Essential Question connects to the unit Big Idea: Economics affects choices.

Differentiated Instruction

▶ **Approaching** Have students look at the illustrations on pages 86-87.

Ask: *What makes these things goods?*

▶ **Beyond** Instruct students to pick a good in the classroom and write a paragraph about the good. Have them include where the good comes from and who might make the good. Ask them to share with the class.

▶ **ELL** Write the word *good* on the board. Discuss the different meanings of *good* (an item that is made for sale, a feeling, a positive outcome). Emphasize the meaning of *good* in this context.

Active Teaching

Words To Know Have students look through the lesson to find the words that are listed in the Word Hunt. Have them read the definitions of the content vocabulary words and use context clues or the glossary to determine the meanings of the academic vocabulary words. Define the academic vocabulary word *provide* for students. Ask students what their parents or caregivers provide for them.

Develop Comprehension

Read and discuss the pages together. Guide students through the written activities. Discuss their responses.

Ask:

1. *What are some goods that are grown?* (corn, strawberries, and beans) **L1**

2. *Where are goods made?* (Answers might include in a building, on land, etc.) **L2**

3. *How might the goods people grow be different from the goods people make?* (Grown goods are from a farm or land; made goods are made by people instead of grown.) **L3**

netw⊚rks

Go to **connected.mcgraw-hill.com** for additional resources:
- Interactive Whiteboard Lessons
- Worksheets
- Assessment
- Content Library

What are services?

A **service** is work done to help others. Service jobs help meet people's needs and wants.

School workers, such as custodians, are service workers. They are paid for the services they do. They sweep the floors and clean the tables. Firefighters and police officers are also service workers. They risk their lives to keep us safe.

> 🖍 Draw or glue pictures of service workers below. Label your pictures.

What service do these firefighters provide?

Some businesses, like gas stations, **provide** both goods and services. A gas station sells goods like gas, oil, and maps. The station also provides a service when it sells its goods.

List other goods and services a gas station might provide. _____

Think of another business that provides both goods and services. Then fill in the chart with the goods and services it provides.

Name of Business: _____

Goods	Services

Lesson 1

❓ Essential Question Why are goods and services important?

_____

Go back to *Show As You Go!* on pages 78–79.

netw⚙rks There's More Online! ▶ Games ▶ Assessment

Active Teaching

Read and discuss the pages together. Ask students to describe a time they used a good or service.

Develop Comprehension

Ask:

1. *What is a service?* (work done to help others) **L1**

2. *How do teachers and firefighters help others?* (Teachers help students learn; firefighters help put out fires.) **L2**

3. *What is the difference between a good and a service?* (Goods are grown or made and services are performed by people) **L3**

Summarize the lesson with the class. Then have students respond to the Essential Question. Discuss students' responses. Have students revisit their response on page 86 and compare it to their response at the end of the lesson. Discuss how their answers may have changed.

Use the leveled reader, *Jobs at School*, to extend and enrich students' understanding of service workers in schools. A lesson plan for this leveled reader can be found on pages T26–T27 at the front of this Teacher Edition.

> ***Show As You Go!*** Remind students to go back to the Unit Opener and complete the activities for this lesson.

Response to Intervention

❓ Essential Question **Why are goods and services important?**

If . . . students have difficulty answering the Essential Question, "Why are goods and services important?"

. . . .

Then . . . take students back to pages 86-88. Discuss how the content relates to the Essential Question.

Ask: *Why do we need goods? Why do we need services?* Following the discussion, allow students to respond to the Essential Question again.

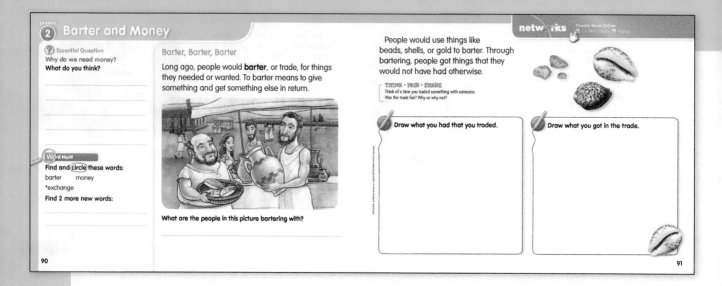

Lesson 2

Activate Prior Knowledge

Show the students different types of money, both bills and coins. Ask them to identify the bills and coins and their values.

Say: *In this lesson, we are going to learn about different kinds of money and why we use it instead of bartering.*

Ask: *Who has ever used money to buy something? How did you know how much it cost? How did you know if you had enough money to buy the item?*

Guide students through the written activities. Discuss their responses.

(?) Essential Question Why do we need money?

Have students explain what they understand about the Essential Question. Discuss their responses. Explain that everything they learn in this lesson will help them understand the Essential Question better. Remind them to think about how the Essential Question connects to the unit Big Idea: Economics affects choices.

More About Money Explain that there has to be something that everyone agrees upon to be our "money" and the value of that "money." Students often believe that money itself is the valuable thing and don't recognize that dollar bills are just paper and coins are just pieces of metal. Students accept the names of the coins without realizing there is an implied meaning in the word itself. For instance, students may not be aware that nickels are called nickels because they used to be made from a precious metal called nickel. Also, quarters are called quarters because they are one-fourth of a dollar. At an early age, students assume that the largest coin is worth the most. They later learn that a small coin can be more valuable than a larger one.

Active Teaching

Words To Know Have students look through the lesson to find the words that are listed in the Word Hunt. Have them read the definitions of the content vocabulary words and use context clues or the glossary to determine the meaning of the academic vocabulary word.

Ask students to look at the spread. Have them use the pictures and heading to predict what the lesson will be about. As they read, have them think about how they use money.

Develop Comprehension

Read pages 90 and 91 together. Guide students through the written activities. Discuss their responses.

Ask:

1. *What does barter mean?* (to give something and get something else in return) **L1**

2. *What did people barter with long ago?* (beads, shells, or gold) **L2**

3. *Why did people barter long ago?* (to get things they would not otherwise have because they didn't have money) **L2**

Differentiated Instruction

▶ **ELL** Write *barter* on the board. Ask students to discuss what they know about bartering long ago. Have them provide a definition for the term barter and discuss how it is similar to trade.

Money, Money, Money

Ana and Sally have **money**. Money is something we use, or **exchange**, to buy goods and services. Money can be paper bills or coins.

Draw what Ana and Sally did to earn their money.

Ana and Sally want to go shopping with their money. Where can they buy a doll?

toy store

What two goods are Ana and Sally looking at?

a big and small doll

Which one costs less money? Circle it!

What are Ana and Sally doing?

using money to buy a doll

What is the man doing?

taking their money in exchange for the doll

At last! Ana and Sally can enjoy their new doll!

Reading Skill

Sequence Place the images below in the order they should happen. Put a number 1, 2, or 3 next to each picture.

2

3

1

Active Teaching

Read and discuss the pages together. Have students look at the spread. As they read, have them think about the times they have used money. Guide students as they complete the activities on each page. Discuss the story sequence.

Develop Comprehension

Ask:

1. *What is money?* (something we use, or exchange, to buy goods and services) **L1**

2. *What did the girls in the story do with their money?* (They bought a doll.) **L2**

3. *Why is money important?* (We need it to buy goods and services.) **L2**

☑ Formative Assessment

Use this assessment to monitor student understanding and identify need for intervention.

• Have students fill out a web about money. On the spokes of the web, have them tell what money is, what it looks like, how it is used, and why it is important.

Reading Skill

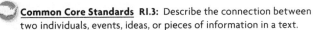

Common Core Standards RI.3: Describe the connection between two individuals, events, ideas, or pieces of information in a text.

Sequencing For additional practice, have partners make up sequence pictures of their own. Switch and have each partner number the sequence in order.

Differentiated Instruction

▶ **Approaching** Reread the story together. Have students role play shopping for a doll or a bike. Have them retell the story using time order words.

▶ **Beyond** Write and illustrate a paragraph about a shopping experience. Use time order words to signal the sequence of events.

▶ **ELL** Read the selection and have students echo-read. Emphasize key terms like *money, exchange, buy, paper bills,* and *coins.* Have students repeat the terms after you. Have students act out scenarios where they exchange money for a good.

Page Power

FOLDABLES Interact more with the page. Have students create a Notebook Foldable to assist them in developing their understanding of sequence.

1. Provide each student with a copy of Foldable 3A from the Notebook Foldables section at the back of this book.

2. Have students construct the Foldable and glue its anchor tab alongside the Reading Skill on page 93.

3. On the Foldable flaps, have students draw 3 sequence pictures of when they bought something.

4. Under the flaps, have students write what they are doing in each picture.

Unit 3 ▪ Lesson 2 **92–93**

Barter and Money

People still barter today. You might barter with your friends for goods and services. For example, you might exchange a blue bracelet for a purple one your friend has.

Today, most people use money because it is easy to carry around. Use the pictures to the right to complete the activity below.

Place a circle around the things that are easy to carry around.

Place a box around the things that are hard to carry around.

How are bartering and using money the same?
You can get goods and services using

both of them.

How are they different?
Money is easy to carry. Things we

barter with can be too big and heavy.

94

Design your own money! Draw a picture of what your money would look like.

Lesson 2

? Essential Question Why do we need money?

Go back to *Show As You Go!* on pages 78–79.

networks There's More Online!

95

Lesson 2

Active Teaching

In this lesson, students learned how bartering and using money are both the same and different. Review the pages together.

Develop Comprehension

Ask:

1. *What are some examples of how people barter today?* **L3**

2. *How do people pay for goods and services today?* (money) **L2**

3. *Why do you think people invented coins and bills?* (easy to carry around and agreed upon value for each coin or bill) **L3**

Summarize the lesson with the class. Then have students respond to the Essential Question. Discuss students' responses. Have students revisit their response on page 90 and compare it to their response at the end of the lesson. Discuss how their answers may have changed.

> *Show As You Go!* Remind students to go back to the Unit Opener and complete the activities for this lesson.

Response to Intervention

? **Essential Question Why do we need money?**

If . . . students have difficulty answering the Essential Question, "Why do we need money?"

. . . .

Then . . . role-play scenarios in which students spend money in exchange for something they need or want. Have students explain what they were able to get in exchange for the money. Help them to understand that we use money to pay for things we need and want.

Ask: *How do you use money and bartering to get goods and services?*

Following the discussion, allow students to respond to the Essential Question again.

networks

Go to **connected.mcgraw-hill.com** for additional resources:

- Interactive Whiteboard Lessons
- Worksheets
- Assessment
- Videos

My State on the Map

Look at the map. Color your state green. Do any other states touch your state? Color them orange.

How many states touch your state?

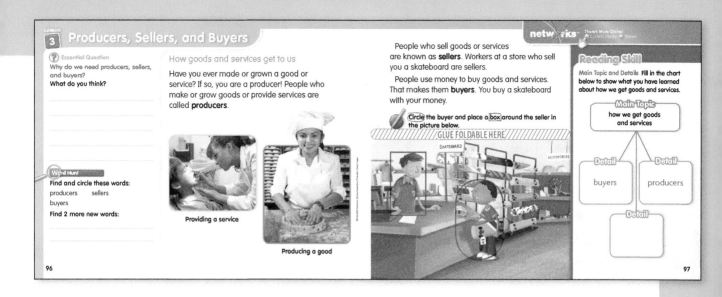

Lesson 3

Activate Prior Knowledge

Engage students in a discussion of producers, sellers, and buyers.

Ask: *Do you know anyone who grows or makes something to sell? What do they grow or make?*

Explain that producers need buyers to buy their goods or services. Buyers need sellers to sell their goods or services to them. Producers, sellers, and buyers all need each other.

Ask: *Did you know that a producer made the chairs you are sitting in? What other goods in our classroom do you think a producer made?*

(?) **Essential Question Why do we need producers, sellers, and buyers?**

Have students explain what they understand about the Essential Question. Discuss their responses. Explain that everything they learn in this lesson will help them understand the Essential Question better. Remind them to think about how the Essential Question connects to the unit Big Idea.

Page Power

FOLDABLES Interact more with the page. Have students create a Notebook Foldable to assist them in developing their understanding of buyers and sellers.

1. Provide each student with a copy of Foldable 3B from the Notebook Foldables section at the back of this book.

2. Have students construct the Foldable and glue its anchor tab above the picture on page 97.

3. Have students write the word *seller* on the left flap and *buyer* on the right flap.

4. On the backs of the flaps, have students draw a picture of a buyer and a seller.

Active Teaching

Words To Know Have students look through the lesson to find the words from the Word Hunt. Have them read the definitions of the content vocabulary words. Have students list examples of producers, sellers, and buyers that they are familiar with.

Develop Comprehension

Read pages 96 and 97 together. Guide students through the written activities. Discuss their responses.

Ask:

1. *What is a producer?* (People who make or grow goods or provide services.) **L1**

2. *What is a seller?* (People who sell goods or services.) **L1**

3. *What is a buyer?* (People who use money to buy goods and services.) **L1**

More About Producers

Say: *Did you know that animals can be producers too? Cows are producers when they make milk. Chickens are producers when they lay eggs. Can you think of any other examples of animals as producers?*

net**w**rks

Go to connected.mcgraw-hill.com for additional resources:
- Interactive Whiteboard Lessons
- Worksheets
- Assessment
- Content Library

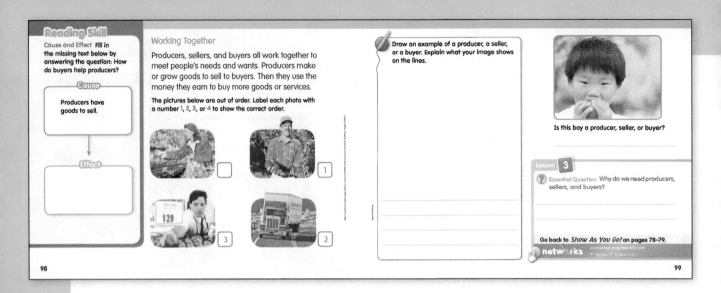

Reading Skill

Cause and Effect **Fill in the missing text below by answering the question: How do buyers help producers?**

Cause

Producers have goods to sell.

Effect

Working Together

Producers, sellers, and buyers all work together to meet people's needs and wants. Producers make or grow goods to sell to buyers. Then they use the money they earn to buy more goods or services.

The pictures below are out of order. Label each photo with a number 1, 2, 3, or 4 to show the correct order.

Draw an example of a producer, a seller, or a buyer. Explain what your image shows on the lines.

Is this boy a producer, seller, or buyer?

Lesson 3

Essential Question Why do we need producers, sellers, and buyers?

Go back to *Show As You Go!* on pages 78–79.

netw**o**rks   connected.mcgraw-hill.com

98   99

Lesson 3

Active Teaching

Have students role play as buyers, sellers, and producers in a school store. Have them pick several goods that will be sold in the store. Assign roles as producers, buyers, and sellers. Help them if there is confusion with the order of producing, buying, and selling the goods.

Develop Comprehension

Ask:

1. *How do producers and sellers work together?* (The producer makes products that a seller will sell.) **L2**

2. *What does a buyer of apples do as a buyer?* (A buyer of apples buys the apples.) **L2**

Summarize the lesson with the class. Then have students respond to the Essential Question. Discuss students' responses. Have students revisit their response on page 96 and compare it to their response at the end of the lesson. Discuss how their answers may have changed.

Use the leveled reader, *The Apple Man: The Story of John Chapman*, to extend and enrich students' understanding of producers, sellers, and buyers. A lesson plan for this leveled reader can be found on pages T28-T29 at the front of this Teacher Edition.

> *Show As You Go!* Remind students to go back to the Unit Opener and complete the activities for this lesson.

Response to Intervention

? **Essential Question** **Why do we need producers, sellers, and buyers?**

If . . . students cannot give a substantiated response to the Essential Question, "Why do we need producers, sellers, and buyers?"

. . . .

Then . . . take students back to pages 96-97. Discuss how the content relates to the Essential Question.
Ask: *How do producers, sellers, and buyers work together to meet our needs and wants?*

Following the discussion, allow students to respond to the Essential Question again.

Reading Skill

Common Core Standards RI.3: Describe the connection between two individuals, events, ideas, or pieces of information in a text.

Cause and Effect For additional practice, have students create a cause and effect chart of their own. Have them create one by answering the question: How do producers help sellers?

netw**o**rks

Go to **connected.mcgraw-hill.com** for additional resources:

- Interactive Whiteboard Lessons
- Worksheets
- Assessment
- Lesson Plans

My State on the Map

Look at the map. Color your state green. Do any other states touch your state? Color them orange.

How many states touch your state?

98–99 Unit 3 • Lesson 3

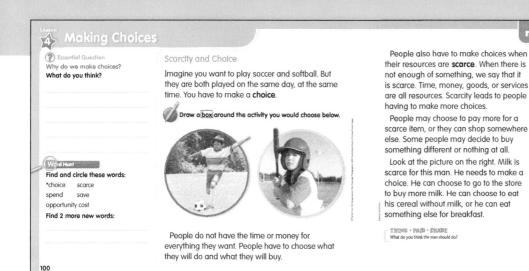

Lesson
4 Making Choices

netw rks There's More Online!
Content Library • Videos

100

101

Essential Question
Why do we make choices?
What do you think?

Word Hunt
Find and circle these words:
*choice   scarce
spend   save
opportunity cost
Find 2 more new words:

Scarcity and Choice

Imagine you want to play soccer and softball. But they are both played on the same day, at the same time. You have to make a **choice**.

Draw a box around the activity you would choose below.

People do not have the time or money for everything they want. People have to choose what they will do and what they will buy.

People also have to make choices when their resources are **scarce**. When there is not enough of something, we say that it is scarce. Time, money, goods, or services are all resources. Scarcity leads to people having to make more choices.

People may choose to pay more for a scarce item, or they can shop somewhere else. Some people may decide to buy something different or nothing at all.

Look at the picture on the right. Milk is scarce for this man. He needs to make a choice. He can choose to go to the store to buy more milk. He can choose to eat his cereal without milk, or he can eat something else for breakfast.

THINK • PAIR • SHARE
What do you think the man should do?

What resource is scarce for this man?
milk

Lesson 4

Activate Prior Knowledge

After students have read and circled their choice on page 100,

Say: *You've probably had to choose between two activities before. There are many other reasons when you might have made a choice. What are some other times you might have to make a decision or choose between two things?*

Explain to students that in this lesson they will be learning about making choices.

Say: *Imagine your class is studying fire trucks. You are given a picture of a fire truck to color in. There are only 5 red crayons for your entire class. What choices do you have to complete your assignment of coloring the fire truck?*

? Essential Question **Why do we make choices?**

Have students explain what they understand about the Essential Question. Discuss their responses. Explain that everything they learn in this lesson will help them understand the Essential Question better. Remind them to think about how the Essential Question connects to the unit Big Idea: Economics affects choices.

Active Teaching

Words To Know Have students look through the lesson to find the words that are listed in the Word Hunt. Have them read the definitions of the content vocabulary words and use context clues or the glossary to determine the meaning of the academic vocabulary word. Then, define the academic vocabulary word *choice* for students.

Say: *When we make a choice, we decide on something.*

Ask students to name a time when they had to make a choice.

Develop Comprehension

Read pages 100 and 101 together. Guide students through the written activities. Discuss their responses.

Ask:

1. *What can you do if water became scarce?* (try to limit use of water) **L3**

2. *Why do we have to make choices?* (because there is not enough money or time to buy or do all the things we want) **L2**

3. *Why can we not buy everything we want?* (We don't have enough money.) **L2**

Differentiated Instruction

▶ **ELL** Write the word *choice* on the board and discuss what the word means. Tell the students they make several choices a day and might not realize it. Examples may be what to pack for lunch, what shirt to wear, or what to watch on TV. Ask them to give you an example of a choice they have made today.

What to choose?

Remember, we have to make choices about time, money, and goods. David makes choices about how to **spend** his money. When he spends his money, he uses it to buy something.

First, David should spend his money on the things he needs, like pencils for school. Then, David can use the rest of his money to buy the things he wants. David wants a new baseball hat.

David may choose to **save** his money instead of buying a baseball hat. To save means to keep your money to spend later. David could save his money in his piggy bank over time. Then he would be able to buy something that costs more!

Match the word with the picture.

save

want

need

102

Time can also be scarce. Imagine that you have a lot of homework to do. You also want to watch your favorite TV show. You will have to choose between doing your homework and watching TV.

You choose to do your homework. Your homework needs to be turned in to your teacher tomorrow. You have to give up watching TV. The thing people give up to do something else is called the **opportunity cost**.

Watching TV is your

o _ _ p o _ t u _ _ _ _ y

c o s _

Lesson 4

? Essential Question Why do we make choices?

_____

_____

Go back to *Show As You Go!* on pages 78–79.

netw*o*rks There's More Online!

103

Lesson 4

Active Teaching

Remind students that we make decisions about how to spend our money and use our time. Have them imagine that they each have $5 to spend.

Say: *What would you spend it on? Would you choose to spend it on candy or save it for later? Why?*

Maybe they want to save it for a new toy or going to the movies. Then the candy would be the opportunity cost.

Develop Comprehension

Ask:

1. *Where can we save our money?* (piggy bank, savings account at a bank, under our pillow, etc.) **L2**

2. *Why is it important to save our money?* (to save for something we really need or want) **L3**

Summarize the lesson with the class. Then have students respond to the Essential Question. Discuss students' responses. Have students revisit their response on page 100 and compare it to their response at the end of the lesson. Discuss how their answers may have changed.

> *Show As You Go!* Remind students to go back to complete the project on the Unit Opener.

Response to Intervention

? **Essential Question** **Why do we make choices?**

If . . . students cannot give a substantiated response to the Essential Question, "Why do we make choices?"

. . . .

Then . . . take students back to pages 100–101. Discuss how the content relates to the Essential Question. Have students think about a time when they had to choose between two or more goods or services.

Ask: *How did you decide what good or service you wanted?*

Allow students to explain how they make choices. Following the discussion, Allow students to respond to the Essential Question again.

netw*o*rks

Go to **connected.mcgraw-hill.com** for additional resources:

- Interactive Whiteboard Lessons
- Worksheets
- Assessment
- Skill Builders

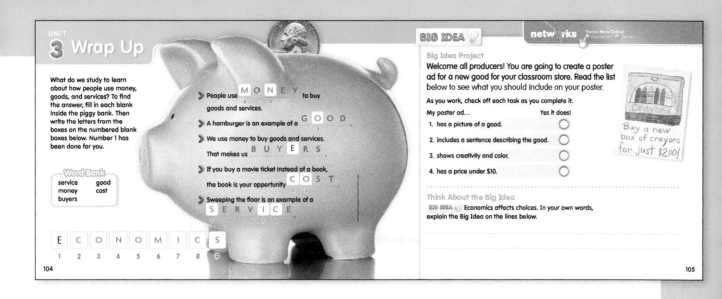

What do we study to learn about how people use money, goods, and services? To find the answer, fill in each blank inside the piggy bank. Then write the letters from the boxes on the numbered blank boxes below. Number 1 has been done for you.

Word Bank
service good
money cost
buyers

> People use M O N E Y to buy goods and services.
> A hamburger is an example of a G O O D .
> We use money to buy goods and services. That makes us B U Y E R S
> If you buy a movie ticket instead of a book, the book is your opportunity C O S T
> Sweeping the floor is an example of a S E R V I C E

E C O N O M I C S
1 2 3 4 5 6 7 8 9

BIG IDEA

Big Idea Project
Welcome all producers! You are going to create a poster ad for a new good for your classroom store. Read the list below to see what you should include on your poster.

As you work, check off each task as you complete it.

My poster ad...   Yes it does!
1. has a picture of a good.   ◯
2. includes a sentence describing the good.   ◯
3. shows creativity and color.   ◯
4. has a price under $10.   ◯

Buy a new box of crayons for just $2.00!

Think About the Big Idea
BIG IDEA Economics affects choices. In your own words, explain the Big Idea on the lines below.

Wrap Up

Fill-in-the-Blank Puzzle

Have students complete the sentences on the pig puzzle page. Then have them answer the question: *What do we study to learn about how people use money, goods, and services?* by writing the letters from the sentences on the numbered blanks at the bottom of the page. Assign partners to check each other's work.

BIG IDEA   Unit Project

Students should refer to the unit opening spread to assist them in completing this project. Students will be making a poster to show what they have learned in Unit 3.

1. Read the checklist together and answer questions students may have about the project.
2. Pass out poster board or large pieces of construction paper. Include crayons, markers, pencils, etc., for the students to use to design their posters.
3. Make sure the students include a sentence about what the good is and what its price is on the poster.
4. Hang the posters in the classroom.
5. After students complete their projects, encourage self-reflection by asking:
   - How did you choose your good?
   - What changes would you make to this poster if you did it again?
6. To assess the project, refer to the rubric on the following page.

Differentiated Instruction

▶ **Approaching** Have students cut out a picture of a good and list its price. Then have them work with a partner to write a sentence describing the good.

▶ **Beyond** Have students write and perform a commercial for the good.

▶ **ELL** Have students work with a partner to write a sentence about their good. Encourage them to talk about the good they pictured on their poster.

Response to Intervention

BIG IDEA   Economics affects choices.

If . . . students cannot give a substantiated response to the Big Idea, "Economics affects choices"

Then . . . remind them that they cannot choose to buy everything they want. Ask them to remember why this is and why we need to make choices about our time and money.

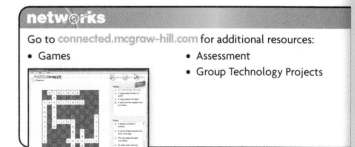

networks

Go to connected.mcgraw-hill.com for additional resources:
- Games
- Assessment
- Group Technology Projects

Name _____ Date _____

Economics Poster Rubric

4 Exemplary	3 Accomplished	2 Developing	1 Beginning
The poster:	**The poster:**	**The poster:**	**The poster:**
☐ accurately uses words and pictures to show a good from the classroom	☐ uses mostly accurate words and pictures to show a good from the classroom	☐ uses some accurate words and pictures to show a good from the classroom	☐ uses few accurate words and pictures to show a good from the classroom
☐ accurately uses words and pictures to show a price under $10 for the good	☐ uses mostly accurate words and pictures to show a price under $10 for the good	☐ uses some accurate words and pictures to show a price under $10 for the good	☐ uses few accurate words and pictures to show a price under $10 for the good
☐ accurately uses words and pictures to show creativity and color	☐ uses mostly accurate words and pictures to show creativity and color	☐ uses some accurate words and pictures to show creativity and color	☐ uses few accurate words and pictures to show creativity and color
☐ contains few, if any, errors in grammar, punctuation, capitalization, and spelling	☐ contains some errors in grammar, punctuation, capitalization, and spelling	☐ contains several errors in grammar, punctuation, capitalization, and spelling	☐ contains serious errors in grammar, punctuation, capitalization, and spelling

Grading Comments: _____

_____

_____

_____

_____

_____

_____

_____

Project Score: _____

Teacher Notes

UNIT
4 Planner GOOD CITIZENS

 **BIG IDEA** 💡 **People's actions affect others.**

Student Portfolio

- **Show As You Go!**
  Use these pages to introduce the Big Idea. Students record information specific to each lesson. They use these pages to help them plan their Big Idea Project.

netw⊙rks

- **Group Technology Project**
  Students use 21ˢᵗ century skills to complete a group extension activity of the unit project. Lesson plans, worksheets, and rubrics are available online.

Student Portfolio

- **Big Idea Project**
  Students will perform a "Good Citizens" skit that shows others how to be good citizens. The Big Idea Project rubric is on page 141W.

Reading Skills

Student Portfolio

- **Reading Skill: Identify Author's Reasons**
  Pages 108–109. Common Core State Standards RI.8

netw⊙rks

- **Skill Builders**
  Introduce and practice the reading skill.

Leveled Readers

Use the leveled reader *Jane Addams and the House That Helped* with Lesson 3. Find the lesson plan on pages T30–T31 of your Teacher Edition.

Treasures Connection

Teach this unit with Treasures Unit 2, *Signs We See*, pages 144–147.

Social Studies Skills

Student Portfolio

- **Primary Sources: Video and Audio Recordings**
  Page 113

netw⊙rks

- **Skill Builders**
  Introduce and teach analyzing primary sources.

Activity Cards

- **Center for Social Studies Skills Investigation**
  Use the center activity cards to help students explore Primary Sources, Geography, and Citizenship.

FOLDABLES®

Student Portfolio

- Students can create vocabulary Foldables right in their portfolios.
- Additional Foldables templates can be found on pages R1–R8 of your Teacher Edition.

Assessment Solutions

- **McGraw-Hill networks™**
  Safe online testing features multiple question types that are easy to use and editable!
- **Self-Check Quizzes**
- **Worksheets**

UNIT 4 **At a Glance**

Lesson	Essential Question	Vocabulary	Digital Resources
1 We Are Citizens	What does it mean to be a good citizen?	citizen rule law right responsibility *belong	Go to connected.mcgraw-hill.com for additional resources: • Interactive Whiteboard Lessons
2 People and Authority	How can people's actions affect others?	authority government conflict *decision	• Worksheets • Assessment
3 Good Citizens Help	How can citizens make a difference?	service project *activity	• Lesson Plans • Content Library • Skill Builders
4 Symbols of Our Country	How do people and symbols stand for America?	symbol democracy *pledge	• Videos • Use Standards Tracker on **networks** to track students' progress.

*denotes academic vocabulary

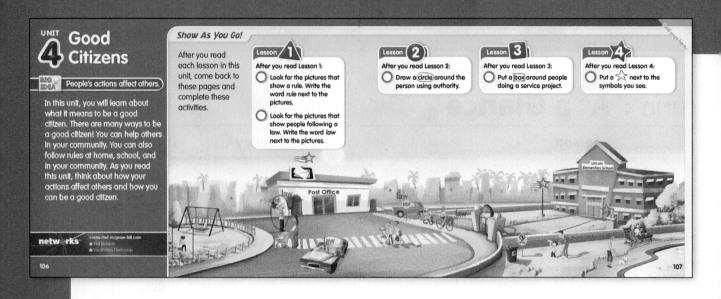

Introduce the Unit

☑ Diagnostic Assessment

Have students work in teams of four or five students. Follow these steps for a brief assessment:

- Give teams an index card for each of the following topics: home, school, and community.
- Have students write two or three ways people can show good citizenship on their index cards.
- Then hold a class discussion to get responses from each team.

Your assessment should be based on how much each student contributes to the team discussion and the whole-class discussion.

Say: *In this unit, we are going to learn about how people can be good citizens at school and in their communities.*

Active Teaching

BIG IDEA   **People's actions affect others.**
In this unit, students will learn what it means to be a good citizen. Students will use the *Show As You Go!* pages throughout their study of this unit. As they read each lesson, students will use information from the lesson to complete these pages.

At this point, have students fold back the corner of page 107. This will help them flip back to this page as needed. Explain to students that at the end of the unit, they will use the information collected on these pages to complete their Big Idea Project.

Differentiated Instruction

▶ **Approaching** Review the directions with students and help define any unfamiliar words. After each lesson, allow students to work in a small group to complete the activity.

▶ **Beyond** Have students write a caption at the bottom of the page that describes how people can be good citizens.

▶ **ELL** Read the directions to students. Define any unfamiliar words. Then have students look over the illustration on pages 106–107 and describe what is happening. As students complete the lessons, allow them to work with a partner to discuss and record information on these pages.

Reading Skill

Common Core Standards
RI.8 Identify reasons an author gives to support points in a text.

Identify Author's Reasons

Authors, or writers, usually have a purpose for writing. They may want readers to think about something important or do something. Authors support these points by giving reasons.

As you read, think about whether the reasons support the author's point.

108

Learn It

To help you identify an author's reasons:

1. Read the story. Identify the author's main point.
2. Ask yourself: What does the author want me to think about or do?
3. Read the story again. Find the reasons that support the author's main point.

It is important to pick up trash on our beaches. Trash makes our beaches look dirty and ugly. Trash can be dangerous. It can kill and harm our sea animals. Trash is also bad for the environment. Let's keep our beaches clean and safe!

> This is the author's point.

> This is one reason that supports the author's main point. Underline two more reasons.

Try It

Write the author's point and reasons from the story on page 108 in the chart the below.

Author's Point
It is important to pick up trash on our beaches.

Reason
Trash makes our beaches look dirty and ugly.

Reason
Trash can be dangerous.

Reason
Trash is also bad for the environment.

Apply It

Read the story below. Circle the author's point. Underline three reasons.

Planting a garden is good for many reasons. It can help you relax. It is good exercise. But most of all, a garden will give you fresh fruits and vegetables. All this is good for your health!

Common Core Standards RI.8 Identify the reasons an author gives to support points in a text.

Reading Skill

Active Teaching

LEARN IT Identify Author's Reasons

Read the first paragraph on page 108 together. Explain that writers use reasons to support what they write. Share this reading strategy:

Say: *As I read a story, I look for the author's point. This tells me what the author wants me to think about or do. Then, I look for the reasons the author uses to support his or her point. Finally, I ask myself if the reasons support the point.*

Read the LEARN IT activity together. Discuss the author's point. Then ask students to identify why the author believes it is important to collect trash. Explain that these are the reasons.

TRY IT Encourage students to try the modeled strategy as they complete the TRY IT activity.

APPLY IT Have students complete the APPLY IT activity.

Ask:

1. *What is the author's point?* (Planting a garden is good for many reasons.) **L1**
2. *What reasons does the author give to support the main point?* (It can help you relax. It is good exercise. A garden will give you fresh fruits and vegetables.) **L2**
3. *Why is it important to identify an author's reasons?* (Identifying the reasons helps readers determine whether the author supports his or her point.) **L3**

Differentiated Instruction

▶ **Approaching** Review the LEARN IT activity as a small group. Do the TRY IT activity together. Have students complete the APPLY IT activity independently. Re-group to compare and correct students' answers.

▶ **Beyond** Ask students to write a short paragraph that includes a main point and two or three reasons that support the point. Then have students trade their paragraphs and use the graphic organizer to identify the main points and reasons.

▶ **ELL** Read pages 108–109 with students. Go over the strategies in the LEARN IT activity. Help students identify the author's point and the reasons in the paragraph. Guide students as they complete the graphic organizer in the TRY IT activity. Have students work in pairs to complete the APPLY IT activity. Regroup to compare and correct students' answers.

networks

Go to connected.mcgraw-hill.com for additional resources:
- Skill Builders
- Graphic Organizers

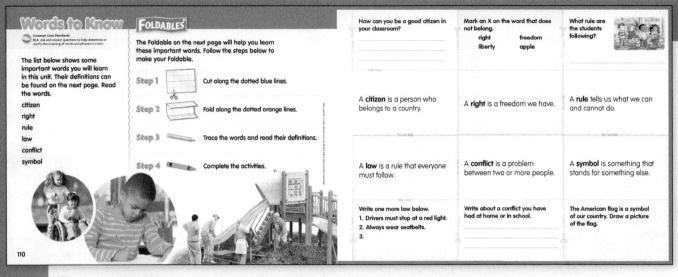

Common Core Standards RI.4 Ask and answer questions to help determine or clarify the meaning of words and phrases in a text.

Words to Know

Active Teaching

FOLDABLES

1. Go to connected.mcgraw-hill.com for flashcards to introduce the unit vocabulary to students.

2. Read the words on the list on page 110 and have students repeat them after you.

3. Guide students as they complete steps 1 through 4 of the Foldable.

4. Have students use the Foldable to practice the vocabulary words independently or with a partner.

networks

Go to connected.mcgraw-hill.com for additional resources:
- Vocabulary Flash-cards
- Vocabulary Games
- Graphic Organizers

GO Vocabulary!

Use the graphic organizer below to help students practice the meaning of the words from the list. Model for students how to complete the graphic organizer using the word *citizen*. Then have students complete the graphic organizer for the other words independently or with a partner.

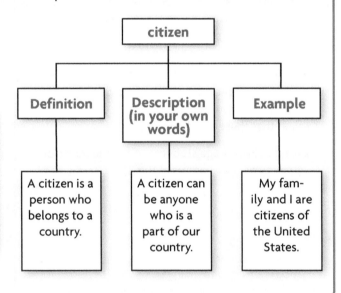

citizen

Definition	Description (in your own words)	Example
A citizen is a person who belongs to a country.	A citizen can be anyone who is a part of our country.	My family and I are citizens of the United States.

FOLDABLES®

Video and audio recordings are primary sources. A video recording is a picture with sound. Movies and TV shows are video recordings. An audio recording is a sound recording without video.

You can learn about people, places, and events by listening to and watching video and audio recordings. Look at the video on the right. It shows a news program about bullies in school.

DBQ Document-Based Questions

1. **What is happening in the video?**
   a girl is being bullied

2. **What advice would you give to the girl who is being bullied?**
   _____
   _____

networks
There's More Online!
● Skill Builders
● Resource Library

113

Differentiated Instruction

▶ **ELL** Say and define the words on page 110. Give one or two examples of each. Then ask students to give their own examples. After you define the word *right*,

Say: *One right we have is the right to go to school. Another right is the right to celebrate religious holidays.*

W O R D   P L A Y

Play Wordo to help students practice the vocabulary words from page 110.

- Print the Wordo cards template from connected .mcgraw-hill.com. Make one copy per student and distribute to the class.

- Have students randomly write words from the list on page 110 in each square.

- Orally present a sentence or definition for each word on the list.

- Have students place counters or chips over the word that corresponds with the sentence or definition.

- A player wins when a vertical, horizontal, or diagonal line is covered.

When students are familiar with the game, you may choose to have them take turns calling out the definitions and sentences.

Active Teaching

Begin a discussion by asking how many students watch videos online. Explain that many of these videos are primary sources. Tell students that videos are primary sources because they are documenting life today and can be used to describe this time period. Give students additional examples of video and audio recordings. Some examples include news programs, speeches (audio and video), movies, or songs. If possible, show students a video from this unit from the Learn 360 playlist.

Read and discuss page 113 together. Guide students through the written activities.

Ask: *Why is a video recording a primary source? What can we learn from video and audio recordings?*

networks

Go to connected.mcgraw-hill.com for additional resources:

- **Skill Builders**
- **Resource Library**

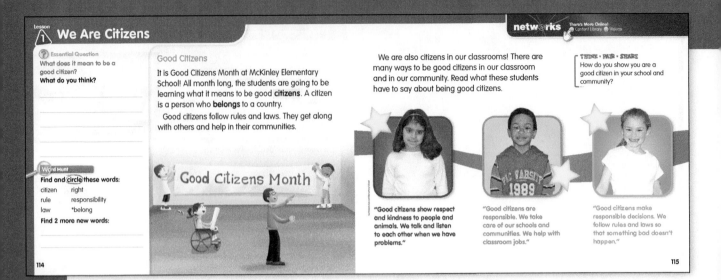

Lesson 1 We Are Citizens

networks There's More Online! Content Library Videos

Essential Question
What does it mean to be a good citizen?
What do you think?

Word Hunt
Find and circle these words:
citizen   right
rule   responsibility
law   *belong
Find 2 more new words:

Good Citizens

It is Good Citizens Month at McKinley Elementary School! All month long, the students are going to be learning what it means to be good **citizens**. A citizen is a person who **belongs** to a country.

Good citizens follow rules and laws. They get along with others and help in their communities.

Good Citizens Month

We are also citizens in our classrooms! There are many ways to be good citizens in our classroom and in our community. Read what these students have to say about being good citizens.

"Good citizens show respect and kindness to people and animals. We talk and listen to each other when we have problems."

"Good citizens are responsible. We take care of our schools and communities. We help with classroom jobs."

"Good citizens make responsible decisions. We follow rules and laws so that something bad doesn't happen."

THINK • PAIR • SHARE
How do you show you are a good citizen in your school and community?

114

115

Lesson 1

Activate Prior Knowledge

Have students do a picture walk through the lesson. Then create a KWL chart on the board. Ask students what they already know about being a good citizen. Then ask them what they want to learn as they read the lesson. List students' responses on the chart. Revisit the chart once students have read the lesson to add information in the last column.

Good Citizens

What I **K**now	What I **W**ant to Learn	What I **L**earned

Say: *In this lesson, we are going to learn about good citizens. We will also learn about the rights and responsibilities we have and the rules and laws that we follow.*

Essential Question **What does it mean to be a good citizen?**

Have students explain what they understand about the Essential Question. Discuss their responses. Explain that everything they learn in this lesson will help them understand the Essential Question better. Remind them to think about how the Essential Question connects to the unit Big Idea: People's actions affect others.

Active Teaching

Words To Know Have students find the content vocabulary words in the lesson and read the definitions. Define the academic vocabulary word *belong* for students.

Say: *We belong to many groups. We belong to a family. We belong to this school.*

Then ask students to list other groups or places to which they belong.

Develop Comprehension

Read pages 114–115 with students. Guide them through the written activities and discuss their responses.

Ask:

1. *What is a citizen?* **L1**
2. *What do good citizens do to help others?* **L2**
3. *How can you show respect and kindness to people? To animals?* **L2**
4. *Why is it important to be a good citizen?* **L3**

Differentiated Instruction

▶ **ELL** Have students create a picture glossary for the vocabulary words in this lesson. Students can work in pairs to brainstorm ideas for their drawings, or they can work individually. Start by pointing out the word *citizen* on page 114. Say the word and define it. Have students discuss what it means to be a citizen. Finally, have them draw an illustration in their glossaries. Repeat these steps for the remaining words.

Reading Skill

Clarify Words and Phrases
Sometimes you may not understand the meaning of a word. When this happens, read the story again and look for clues. What do the words below mean?

Right:
a freedom we have

Responsibility:
a duty we have

Rights and Responsibilities

Mrs. Garcia's students are learning about **rights** and **responsibilities**. A right is a freedom we have. We have the right to go to school and to be safe in school.

The students learn that a responsibility is a duty we have. We have the responsibility to come to school on time. It is also our responsibility to throw away litter, or trash, and to keep our schools and communities clean.

Mrs. Garcia asked her students to put together a list of ways to be responsible citizens in school. Look at their list below.

Think of one more way to be responsible at school. Write it down next to the red star.

Responsible Citizens

★ Follow rules

★ Respect others

★ Arrive to school on time

★ Care about the environment

★ _____

Draw a picture that shows one way to be a responsible citizen.

116

117

Active Teaching

Have students complete the following sentence frames:

- At home, I am responsible for _____.
- At school, I am responsible for _____.
- I have a right, or freedom, to _____.

Discuss students' responses. Tell students that they will be learning about the rights and responsibilities they have as citizens. Read and discuss pages 116–117 together. Guide students through the activities. Discuss their responses.

Develop Comprehension

Ask:

1. *How are the children in the pictures on pages 116 and 117 being responsible citizens?* **L1**

2. *Why is it important to have rights?* **L3**

3. *Why is it important to have responsibilities? What would happen if we did not have responsibilities?* **L3**

Reading Skill

 Common Core Standards RI.4 Ask and answer questions to help determine or clarify the meaning of words and phrases in a text.

Clarify Words and Phrases Tell students that sometimes they may come across a word or a phrase they do not understand. Explain that when this happens, they should read the story or text again and look for clues. Point to the words *rights* and *responsibilities*. Have students read each paragraph aloud. Then ask them to write what they think the words mean.

Differentiated Instruction

▶ **Approaching** Read the selection with students. As students read each paragraph, help them identify and underline important words, phrases, and sentences. If students are allowed to use a highlighter, have them use one in place of a pencil.

▶ **Beyond** Have students read pages 116–117. Ask students to write a one or two-sentence summary for each paragraph.

▶ **ELL** Have students work in pairs or small groups to read the selection. Ask them to role-play the traits of a good citizen listed on page 117. Then have students explain in their own words what the words *rights* and *responsibilities* mean to them.

Today, Mrs. Garcia's class is learning about **rules**. "Rules tell us what we can and cannot do," she says. Mrs. Garcia reminds students that we follow rules at home, such as picking up after ourselves.

"We also follow rules in school. Rules keep order and help us to stay safe. One school rule is to wait our turn in line. This rule makes things fair for everyone," says Mrs. Garcia.

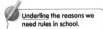 Underline the reasons we need rules in school.

"We need rules in the classroom, too," says Mrs. Garcia. "One classroom rule is to raise our hands when we want to speak. This rule gives everyone in class a turn to speak and be heard."

"Can someone give me an example of another rule?" asks Mrs. Garcia. Julia raises her hand and says, "One rule is to respect each other and our belongings."

Mrs. Garcia needs one more rule. Can you think of a good rule for her class? Write it on the poster next to 4.

//////// GLUE FOLDABLE HERE ////////
Mrs. Garcia's
Classroom Rules

1. Raise our hands to talk.

2. Be kind to each other.

3. Take turns.

4. _____

118

119

Lesson 1

Active Teaching

Begin a discussion about the importance of rules. Ask students to think about places in the community where rules are important (for example, community swimming pools, school playground, parks, libraries, and hospitals).

Ask: *What would happen if we did not have rules?*

Read and discuss pages 118–119 together. Guide students through the written activities.

Develop Comprehension

Ask:

1. *What rules do we follow in class? In school?* **L1**

2. *What rules do you follow at home?* **L1**

3. *Why is it important to walk, and not run, indoors?* **L2**

4. *Why do we need rules?* (Rules help us keep order and make things fair for everyone. Rules also keep us safe.) **L3**

Differentiated Instruction

▶ **Approaching** Allow students to work in pairs. Have them take turns reading the lesson. Then ask them to illustrate the rules they read about in the lesson. Have them write captions for their illustrations.

▶ **Beyond** Have students work in pairs or small groups to discuss the causes and effects of not following rules. Encourage them to talk about what might happen if each rule in the lesson were not followed. Work with groups to organize cause-and-effect relationships on a chart.

▶ **ELL** Have students read the selection aloud. Ask them to stop after each paragraph and summarize what they have read (either verbally or in writing next to the paragraph).

Page Power

FOLDABLES Interact more with the page. Have students create a Notebook Foldable to assist them in developing their understanding of the purpose of rules.

- Provide students with a copy of Foldable 4A from the Notebook Foldables section at the back of this book.

- Have students cut out the Foldable and glue its anchor tab where indicated on page 119.

- On the Foldable flaps, have students write at least four classroom rules they follow.

- On the other side of the Foldable, have them write the consequences of breaking, or not following, the rules.

Laws In Our Community

The next day, Mrs. Garcia's class talks about **laws**. Mrs. Garcia explains that a law is a special kind of rule. "Our leaders make laws that everyone must follow. Like rules, laws also keep order and help us to stay safe."

Carlos raises his hand. He says, "My mom told me it is a law to follow street signs and lights."

"What happens if we do not follow this law?" asks Mrs. Garcia. "Everyone will get into accidents!" the students cry out.

Circle the pictures that show people following traffic laws.

120

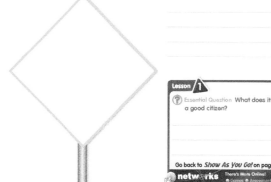
Think of a new law for your community. Draw a picture of your law on the sign.

On the lines below, tell why you think this new law will help your community.

Lesson 1

Essential Question What does it mean to be a good citizen?

Go back to *Show As You Go!* on pages 106–107.

networks There's More Online!
• Games • Assessment

121

Active Teaching

Make copies of signs that show different laws in the community (for example, a stop sign, a no parking sign, a handicapped parking sign, a no littering sign, and so forth). Hold up each image and have students identify the law depicted. Explain that communities have different laws.

Read pages 120–121 together. Have students complete the activities. Discuss their responses.

Develop Comprehension

Ask:

1. *What does the word* law *mean?* **L1**
2. *What are some community laws?* (wear a seatbelt, stop at the stop sign, drive at the green light, do not steal or damage personal properties) **L2**
3. *Why do we need laws?* (Laws help us to stay safe. They also help people get along.) **L3**

Summarize the lesson with the class. Then have students respond to the Essential Question. Discuss their responses. Have students revisit their response on page 114 and compare it to their response at the end of the lesson. Discuss how their answers changed.

> *Show As You Go!* Remind students to go back to the Unit Opener and complete the activities for this lesson.

Response to Intervention

(?) Essential Question **What does it mean to be a good citizen?**

If . . . students cannot give a substantiated response to the Essential Question, "What does it mean to be a good citizen?"

. . . .

Then . . . re-read the lesson with students. After reading each lesson, have students identify the main idea, including what it means to be a good citizen, rights and responsibilities, and rules and laws. Following the discussion, allow students to respond to the Essential Question again.

networks

Go to connected.mcgraw-hill.com for additional resources:
• Interactive Whiteboard Lessons
• Worksheets
• Assessment
• Videos

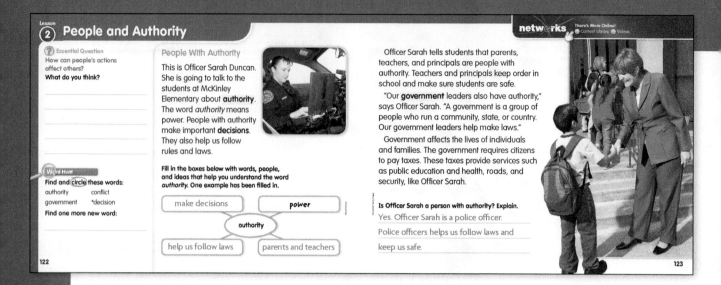

Lesson 2

Activate Prior Knowledge

To pre-assess what students already know, have them respond to the following True and False statements.

- The word *authority* means to be mad or upset.
- People with authority do not have power.
- People with authority have the right to make decisions.
- Bullying is wrong.
- A conflict is a problem.
- You can solve a conflict by not paying attention to it.

Say: *In this lesson, we will learn about people and authority. Authority means power.*

 **Essential Question** **How can people's actions affect others?**

Have students explain what they understand about the Essential Question. Discuss their responses. Explain that everything they learn in this lesson will help them understand the Essential Question better. Remind them to think about how the Essential Question connects to the unit Big Idea: People's actions affect others.

Active Teaching

Words To Know Have students look through the lesson to find the content vocabulary words that are listed in the Word Hunt. Define the academic vocabulary word *decision* for students. Explain that we make decisions every day. We decide what to wear to school each day. Some of us decide what we want to eat for lunch.

Ask: *What kinds of decisions have you made today?*

Develop Comprehension

Read pages 122–123 together. Guide students as they fill in the word web. Encourage them to fill in the web with examples from the text and other examples of people with authority.

Ask:

1. *Who are some people with authority?* (police officers, government leaders, teachers, principals, and parents) **L1**

2. *What can people with authority do to help others?* (They can help others follow rules and laws.) **L2**

3. *What does the word* government *mean?* (people who run a community, a state, or a country) **L1**

Differentiated Instruction

▶ **ELL** Say and define the words *authority*, *government*, and *decision*. To help students understand the meaning of each word, have them role-play a situation where a person with authority makes a decision or helps others follow a rule or law.

People Without Authority

"Sometimes people use power when they do not have authority," explains Officer Sarah. "They may steal something that does not belong to them."

"Some people force others to do things they do not want to do. This is called peer pressure. When you force someone to do something they do not want to do, you are being a bully."

"Using power without authority, can get people into trouble," says Officer Sarah.

Underline two ways people use power without authority.

Read the story "Stop the Bully." Think about how Lola is using power without authority.

Stop the Bully by Eric Johnson

1. Hey, Lisa. Wait up! What's for lunch?
   Umm,...I'm having a turkey sandwich, carrots, and a cookie that my mom made for me.

2. I have a better idea. Why don't you give me the cookie!
   But,...

3. Hey! Move out of the way. It's my turn!
   But, Lola. I've been waiting for it. It's my turn.

4. Is something wrong, Lisa?
   Oh, nothing. I just hurt my knee.

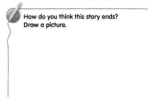

5. No, wait! Miss Smith! Lola has been bullying me, and she won't stop. I don't know what to do.
   Bullying is wrong, Lisa. It is against our rules. I'll take care of it.

How do you think this story ends? Draw a picture.

Active Teaching

Say: *Today, we are going to read a story about a bully. Has anyone ever seen someone being bullied by another person? What happened?*

Allow students to respond to the questions. Following the discussion, explain that bullying is one example of using power without authority. If your school has specific rules about bullying, go over the rules.

As an optional, or additional, activity, have students view a video about bullying from the Learn 360 playlist. Hold a discussion after the viewing.

Develop Comprehension

Read the pages together. Encourage students to perform a dramatization of the story "Stop the Bully." Assign the roles of Lola, Lisa, and Miss Smith. Hold a discussion after the reading to see how students would feel if they were Lisa.

Ask:

1. *What are three examples of using power without authority?* (bullying, stealing, peer pressure) **L1**

2. *What happens in the story, "Stop the Bully"?* (Lola bullies Lisa into giving up her lunch. Lola then bullies Lisa in the playground. Lisa talks to Miss Smith about the situation, and Miss Smith tells Lisa she will help.) **L2**

3. *Why do you think people misuse authority?* **L3**

Page Power

Interact more with the page. Have students:

- underline the meaning of peer pressure.
- write in the margin on page 124 about how stealing something is using power without authority.
- write a caption or fill in speech bubbles to tell how the story ends.
- write the word *bully* next to the person who is a bully.

✅ Formative Assessment

To quickly assess whether students understand the material on pages 122–125, choose one of the following assessment options:

- Provide students with an Exit Card. You can use an index card or a sticky note. Ask students to write a quick response explaining why using power without authority is wrong.
- Ask students to write a brief summary of what they have read about on pages 122–125.
- Have students use a compare and contrast graphic organizer to write about the use of power with and without authority.

Solving Conflicts

A **conflict** is a problem between two or more people. In the story you just read, the conflict is between Lola and Lisa. Lola is a bully. Her actions are hurting Lisa.

There are many ways to solve a conflict. Look at the poster below. It shows ways to solve conflicts.

How to Solve Conflicts

Talk	• Talk to the person you have a conflict with.
	• Tell him or her what you feel is the problem.
Share	• Don't be afraid to share your feelings.
Listen	• Listen to the other person's thoughts and feelings.
Role play	• Ask someone to help you role play how to solve the conflict.

Sometimes, you may need to ask an adult to help you solve a conflict. In the story, Lisa talked to her teacher about the problems she was having. Teachers, principals, and parents can help solve conflicts.

THINK • PAIR • SHARE
Think about a conflict you have had. How did you solve it? Work with a buddy to talk about a conflict you had and how you solved it.

Lesson ②

? Essential Question How do people's actions affect others?

_____

_____

Go back to *Show As You Go!* on pages 106–107.

networks There's More Online!
● Games ● Assessment

126

127

Lesson 2

Active Teaching

Lead a classroom discussion by asking students if they have ever had a conflict with someone.

Ask: *How did you solve the conflict?*

Read and discuss pages 126–127 together. Guide students through the steps on the chart on page 126. Discuss each step with students. If possible, ask volunteers to role-play a conflict and the steps they would use to solve the conflict.

Develop Comprehension

Ask:

1. *What does the word* conflict *mean?* **L1**

2. *How can you solve conflicts?* (talking, sharing, listening, role-palying) **L1**

3. *What advice would you give to someone who is having a conflict?* **L2**

Summarize the lesson with the class. Then have students respond to the Essential Question. Discuss their responses. Have students revisit their response on page 122 and compare it to their response at the end of the lesson. Discuss how their answers changed.

> ***Show As You Go!*** Remind students to go back to the Unit Opener and complete the activities for this lesson.

Response to Intervention

? **Essential Question How can people's actions affect others?**

If . . . students cannot give a substantiated response to the Essential Question, "How can people's actions affect others?"

. . . .

Then . . . re-read or have students role-play the story "Stop the Bully." Ask students to think about how Lola's actions affect Lisa. Following the discussion, allow students to respond to the Essential Question again.

netw⊚rks

Go to connected.mcgraw-hill.com for additional resources:
- Interactive Whiteboard Lessons
- Worksheets
- Assessment
- Videos

My State on the Map
Look at the map. Color your state green. Do any other states touch your state? Color them orange.
How many states touch your state?

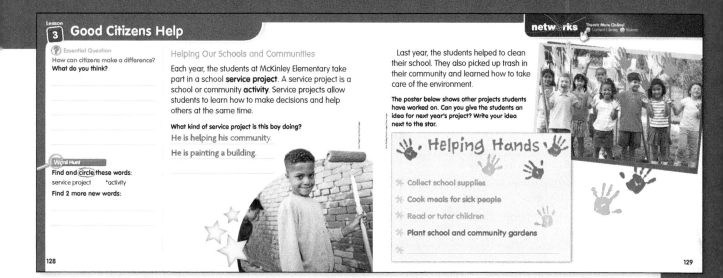

Lesson
3 Good Citizens Help

netw⊕rks There's More Online!
Content Library ● Videos

Essential Question
How can citizens make a difference?
What do you think?

_____

_____

_____

Word Hunt
Find and (circle) these words:
service project   *activity
Find 2 more new words:

128

Helping Our Schools and Communities

Each year, the students at McKinley Elementary take part in a school **service project**. A service project is a school or community **activity**. Service projects allow students to learn how to make decisions and help others at the same time.

What kind of service project is this boy doing?
He is helping his community.

He is painting a building.

_____

Last year, the students helped to clean their school. They also picked up trash in their community and learned how to take care of the environment.

The poster below shows other projects students have worked on. Can you give the students an idea for next year's project? Write your idea next to the star.

Helping Hands

❋ Collect school supplies

❋ Cook meals for sick people

❋ Read or tutor children

❋ Plant school and community gardens

❋ _____

129

Lesson 3

Activate Prior Knowledge

Define the term _service project_. Explain that many people participate in service projects to help others. Give some examples (collecting school supplies, delivering food to people who can't leave their homes, volunteering to help build homes, volunteering at local hospitals or soup kitchens, and planting gardens).

Ask: _What kinds of service projects have you or your family participated in?_

List students' responses on the board or on chart paper.

Say: _In this lesson, we will read about ways that citizens can make a difference in their school and communities._

? **Essential Question How can citizens make a difference?**

Have students explain what they understand about the Essential Question. Discuss their responses. Explain that everything they learn in this lesson will help them understand the Essential Question better. Remind them to think about how the Essential Question connects to the unit Big Idea: People's actions affect others.

Active Teaching

Words To Know Plan a Think, Pair, Share activity by having pairs find the academic vocabulary word _activity_. Say and define the word. Have students list school and community activities in which they participate. Explain that the activities can be extra-curricular activities like soccer, ballet, or baseball.

Develop Comprehension

Read pages 128–129 together. Guide students through the written activities.

Ask:

1. _What is a service project?_ **L1**

2. _What can we learn from service projects?_ (Service projects allow people to make decisions and help others.) **L2**

3. _How can you help your school? How can you help your community?_ **L3**

Differentiated Instruction

▶ **ELL** Write the term _service project_ on the board or on chart paper. Say and define the term. Give examples of service projects in school and in the community. Then ask students to think of other examples of service projects. List students' responses on the board. Discuss why service projects are good for schools and communities.

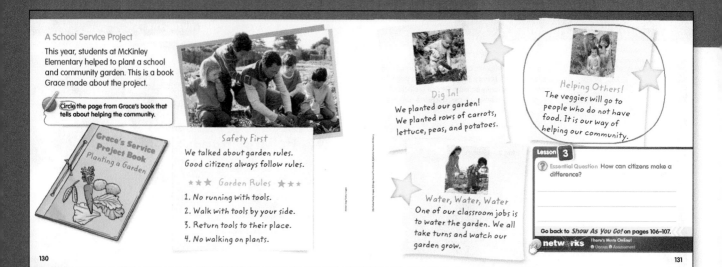

A School Service Project

This year, students at McKinley Elementary helped to plant a school and community garden. This is a book Grace made about the project.

Circle the page from Grace's book that tells about helping the community.

Grace's Service Project Book
Planting a Garden

Safety First
We talked about garden rules. Good citizens always follow rules.

★ ★ ★ Garden Rules ★ ★ ★
1. No running with tools.
2. Walk with tools by your side.
3. Return tools to their place.
4. No walking on plants.

Dig In!
We planted our garden! We planted rows of carrots, lettuce, peas, and potatoes.

Water, Water, Water
One of our classroom jobs is to water the garden. We all take turns and watch our garden grow.

Helping Others!
The veggies will go to people who do not have food. It is our way of helping our community.

Lesson **3**
? Essential Question How can citizens make a difference?

Go back to *Show As You Go!* on pages 106–107.

netw⊕rks There's More Online!
⊕ Games ⊕ Assessment

Lesson 3

Active Teaching

Read and discuss pages 130–131. Guide students as they read Grace's book.

Develop Comprehension

Ask:

1. *What school service project did the students at McKinley Elementary participate in?* **L1**

2. *What kinds of decisions did the students make when planting their garden?* (They decided what rules they would need to follow, what kinds of seeds to plant, where to plant their garden, and how to take care of their garden.) **L3**

3. *How do service projects help people, schools, and communities?* **L3**

Summarize the lesson with the class. Then have students respond to the Essential Question. Discuss students' responses. Have students revisit their response on page 128 and compare it to their response at the end of the lesson. Discuss how their answers changed.

Use the leveled reader, *Jane Addams and the House That Helped*, to extend and enrich students' understanding of how individuals can make a difference. A lesson plan for this leveled reader can be found on pages T30-T31 at the front of this Teacher Edition.

> *Show As You Go!* Remind students to go back to the Unit Opener to complete the activities for this lesson.

Response to Intervention

? **Essential Question How can citizens make a difference?**

If . . . students cannot give a substantiated response to the Essential Question, "How can citizens make a difference?"

. . . .

Then . . . ask students to think about the school service projects discussed in the lesson. Create a two-column chart with the word "School" in one column and the word "Community" in the other column. Have children look through the lesson and list service projects that go under each column. Discuss how each project helps the school or community. Following the discussion, allow students to respond to the Essential Question again.

netw⊕rks

Go to connected.mcgraw-hill.com for additional resources:
- Interactive Whiteboard Lessons
- Worksheets
- Assessment

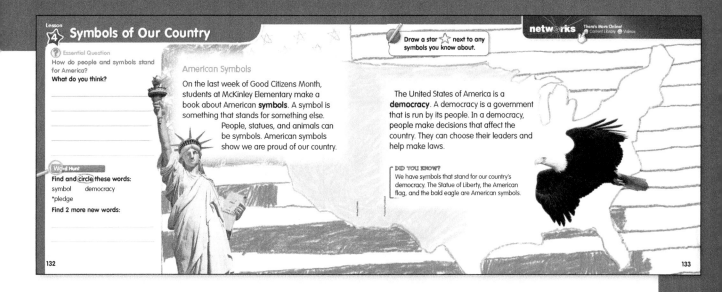

Lesson 4 · Symbols of Our Country

Essential Question
How do people and symbols stand for America?
What do you think?

Word Hunt
Find and circle these words:
symbol   democracy
*pledge
Find 2 more new words:

American Symbols
On the last week of Good Citizens Month, students at McKinley Elementary make a book about American **symbols**. A symbol is something that stands for something else. People, statues, and animals can be symbols. American symbols show we are proud of our country.

Draw a star ☆ next to any symbols you know about.

networks There's More Online!
Content Library Videos

The United States of America is a **democracy**. A democracy is a government that is run by its people. In a democracy, people make decisions that affect the country. They can choose their leaders and help make laws.

DID YOU KNOW?
We have symbols that stand for our country's democracy. The Statue of Liberty, the American flag, and the bald eagle are American symbols.

132

133

Lesson 4

Activate Prior Knowledge

Lead a symbols hunt to see which American symbols students can identify. Give students a sheet of paper. Have them walk around the room and list the symbols they recognize. To prepare ahead of time, hang photos or bring in small replicas of the following symbols:

- American flag
- Statue of Liberty
- bald eagle
- President Lincoln
- Washington Memorial

Go over the correct answers with students.

Say: *In this lesson, we will learn about symbols and people that stand for our country.*

? Essential Question How do people and symbols stand for America?

Have students explain what they understand about the Essential Question. Discuss their responses. Explain that everything they learn in this lesson will help them understand the Essential Question better. Remind them to think about how the Essential Question connects to the unit Big Idea: People's actions affect others.

Active Teaching

Words To Know Have students find the words *symbol* and *democracy* in the text and underline the definitions. Discuss the meanings of each word. If students have trouble understanding the meaning of *democracy*, explain that in a constitutional democracy, citizens can vote for their leaders and laws.

Then define the academic vocabulary word *pledge* (to make a promise). Ask students to think about a time when they made a pledge.

Ask: *Have you ever made a pledge, or a promise? What did you pledge to do?*

Have students respond to the questions.

Say: *When we say the "Pledge of Allegiance," we make a promise to be loyal to our country.*

Develop Comprehension

Ask:

1. *What does the word* symbol *mean?* **L1**
2. *What symbols are shown on pages 132–133?* **L2**
3. *What do American symbols show?* (They show we are proud of our country.) **L2**

Differentiated Instruction

▶ **ELL** Help students understand the meaning of the word *symbol.* Go over each of the symbols in the Activate Prior Knowledge. Give students an index card and have them draw a picture of a symbol on one side of the card. Have students write the name of the symbol and what it stands for on the other side. You might also have students discuss symbols in their native country.

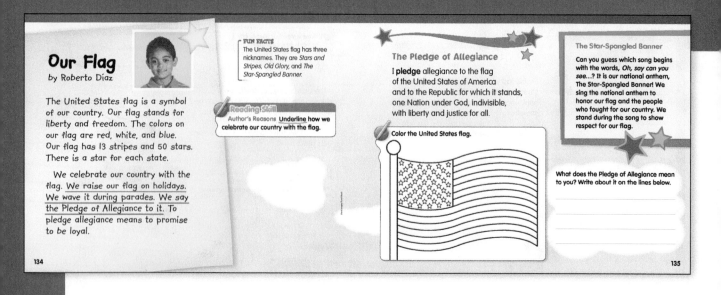

Our Flag
by Roberto Díaz

The United States flag is a symbol of our country. Our flag stands for liberty and freedom. The colors on our flag are red, white, and blue. Our flag has 13 stripes and 50 stars. There is a star for each state.

We celebrate our country with the flag. We raise our flag on holidays. We wave it during parades. We say the Pledge of Allegiance to it. To pledge allegiance means to promise to be loyal.

FUN FACTS
The United States flag has three nicknames. They are *Stars and Stripes, Old Glory,* and *The Star-Spangled Banner.*

Reading Skill
Author's Reasons <u>Underline</u> how we celebrate our country with the flag.

The Pledge of Allegiance
I **pledge** allegiance to the flag of the United States of America and to the Republic for which it stands, one Nation under God, indivisible, with liberty and justice for all.

Color the United States flag.

The Star-Spangled Banner
Can you guess which song begins with the words, *Oh, say can you see...?* It is our national anthem, The Star-Spangled Banner! We sing the national anthem to honor our flag and the people who fought for our country. We stand during the song to show respect for our flag.

What does the Pledge of Allegiance mean to you? Write about it on the lines below.

134

135

Lesson 4

Active Teaching

Look online in your Teacher Resources to find an audio recording of "The Star-Spangled Banner." Have students listen to the words. Explain that the "Star-Spangled Banner" and the "Pledge of Allegiance" were written to honor the American flag and our democracy.

Read the pages together. Guide students through the activities.

Develop Comprehension

Ask:

1. *What does the American flag stand for?* **L1**

2. *Which two songs honor the American flag?* **L1**

3. *How can we honor the flag?* (We raise the flag during holidays. We say the "Pledge of Allegiance" to it.) **L2**

Differentiated Instruction

▶ **Approaching** Provide students with construction paper. Have them draw or cut out images of the symbols from this lesson. Then have them write two or three details they learned about each symbol on the back of the paper.

▶ **Beyond** Provide students with copies of the lyrics for the "Star-Spangled Banner." Have them learn the lyrics of the song. Then ask them to perform the song for the class and explain what they believe is the significance of the song.

▶ **ELL** Read the "Pledge of Allegiance" with students. Help students understand the meaning of these words:

pledge – promise

allegiance – loyalty, faithfulness, devotion

republic – our government

stands – refers to the flag as a symbol

nation – a group of people

indivisible – not able to be divided

liberty – freedom

justice – fair and just treatment for all

The Statue of Liberty
by Melissa Ling

The Statue of Liberty is a symbol of freedom, hope, and friendship. The Statue of Liberty is in New York City.

Today, people from all over the world visit the Statue of Liberty. The statue stands for friendship because she welcomes everyone.

Reading Skill

Ask and Answer Questions
As you read, think about the key details. Ask and answer questions to make sure you understand what you read.

Why does the Statue of Liberty stand for friendship?
The Statue of Liberty welcomes everyone.

136

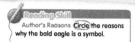

The Bald Eagle
by Aaron Jones, Jr.

When America became a free country, it needed a symbol. Our leaders wanted a symbol to stand for our country's democracy. They chose the bald eagle.

The bald eagle is big and strong. Our country is big and strong, too. The bald eagle stands for a strong, proud, and free America.

Reading Skill

Author's Reasons Circle the reasons why the bald eagle is a symbol.

137

Active Teaching

Read the pages together. Guide students through the activities. Discuss students' responses.

Develop Comprehension

Ask:

1. *Why did our leaders choose the bald eagle as a symbol of our democracy?* (They wanted a symbol that stood for our country's strength and freedom.) **L2**

2. *Why do you think countries have symbols?* (to show they are proud) **L3**

3. *Why are symbols important?* **L3**

Reading Skill

 Common Core Standards **RI.1:** Ask and answer questions about key details in a text.

Ask and Answer Questions

For additional practice, have students work in pairs to re-read the pages together and write two or three questions they have about the text. Bring the class together and discuss students' questions and answers.

Page Power

FOLDABLES Interact more with the page. Have students create a Notebook Foldable to assist them in developing their understanding of symbols.

1. Provide students with a copy of Foldable 4B from the Notebook Foldables section at the back of this book.

2. Have students cut out the Foldable and glue its anchor tab where indicated on page 137.

3. On the Foldable flap, have students compare and contrast the Statue of Liberty and the bald eagle. Ask students to think about what the symbols stand for.

More About the Statue of Liberty The people of France gave the Statue of Liberty to the United States as a token of their friendship and in celebration of the 100th anniversary of America's independence from Great Britain. The statue was split into 350 pieces to ship to the United States. It was reassembled on its pedestal on Bedloe's Island (now Liberty Island) in four months. The seven spikes on the crown stand for the seven continents and the seven seas on our planet. A famous poem carved into the base of the Statue of Liberty welcomes the world's "poor," its "homeless," and its "huddled masses."

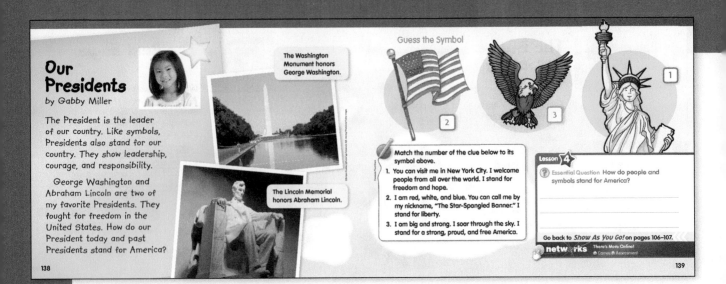

Our Presidents
by Gabby Miller

The President is the leader of our country. Like symbols, Presidents also stand for our country. They show leadership, courage, and responsibility.

George Washington and Abraham Lincoln are two of my favorite Presidents. They fought for freedom in the United States. How do our President today and past Presidents stand for America?

The Washington Monument honors George Washington.

The Lincoln Memorial honors Abraham Lincoln.

Guess the Symbol

Match the number of the clue below to its symbol above.

1. You can visit me in New York City. I welcome people from all over the world. I stand for freedom and hope.

2. I am red, white, and blue. You can call me by my nickname, "The Star-Spangled Banner." I stand for liberty.

3. I am big and strong. I soar through the sky. I stand for a strong, proud, and free America.

Lesson 4

Essential Question How do people and symbols stand for America?

Go back to *Show As You Go!* on pages 106–107.

netw⊚rks There's More Online!
Games • Assessment

138

139

Lesson 4

Active Teaching

Explain that our Presidents also represent, or stand for, America's democracy. Talk about the current President and how he stands for the United States. You may also wish to talk about your favorite President and what the President stands for.

Read and discuss pages 138–139. Guide students as they complete the written activities, except for the Essential Question.

Develop Comprehension

Ask:

1. *How does our President stand for America?* **L2**

2. *What do you know about Abraham Lincoln? What do you know about George Washington?* **L3**

3. *If you were President of the United States, what would you want to stand for?* **L3**

Summarize the lesson with the class. Then have students respond to the Essential Question. Have them revisit their response on page 132 and compare it to their response at the end of the lesson. Discuss how their answers changed.

Show As You Go! Remind students to go back to complete the activities on the Unit Opener.

Response to Intervention

Essential Question **How do people and symbols stand for America?**

If . . . students cannot give a substantiated response to the Essential Question, "How do people and symbols stand for America?"

....

Then . . . revisit pages 134–139. Go over each of the symbols on these pages, making sure that students understand what they stand for. Following the discussion, allow students to respond to the Essential Question again.

netw⊚rks

Go to **connected.mcgraw-hill.com** for additional resources:

- Interactive Whiteboard Lessons
- Worksheets
- Assessment
- Content Library

My State on the Map
Look at the map. Color your state green. Do any other states touch your state? Color them orange.
How many states touch your state?

138–139 Unit 4 ▪ Lesson 4

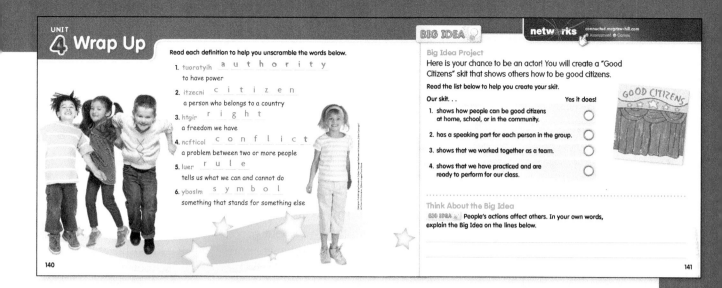

UNIT
4 Wrap Up

Read each definition to help you unscramble the words below.

1. tuoratyih   a u t h o r i t y
   to have power

2. itzecni   c i t i z e n
   a person who belongs to a country

3. htgir   r i g h t
   a freedom we have

4. ncfticol   c o n f l i c t
   a problem between two or more people

5. luer   r u l e
   tells us what we can and cannot do

6. yboslm   s y m b o l
   something that stands for something else

140

BIG IDEA

networks   connected.mcgraw-hill.com
             Assessment ● Games

Big Idea Project
Here is your chance to be an actor! You will create a "Good Citizens" skit that shows others how to be good citizens.

Read the list below to help you create your skit.

Our skit. . .   Yes it does!

1. shows how people can be good citizens
   at home, school, or in the community.   ○

2. has a speaking part for each person in the group.   ○

3. shows that we worked together as a team.   ○

4. shows that we have practiced and are
   ready to perform for our class.   ○

GOOD CITIZENS

Think About the Big Idea
BIG IDEA   People's actions affect others. In your own words,
explain the Big Idea on the lines below.

141

Unit 4 Wrap Up

Word Scramble

Have students complete the activity on page 140 to review the Unit vocabulary. Encourage students to read the definition of each word before writing their answers. If necessary, walk them through the first example.

BIG IDEA   Unit Project

Students will be performing a skit to show what they learned in Unit 4.

1. Read the checklist together and answer any questions students may have about the project.

2. Assign students to groups of four or five students. Ask them to review the lessons in the unit and brainstorm ideas for their skits.

3. Have students perform their skits for the class. Allow students to use a "script" as they perform their skits.

4. After students complete their projects, encourage self-reflection by asking:

   • *What did you like best about performing the skit?*

   • *What did you learn about yourself and others?*

5. To assess the project, refer to the rubric on the following page.

Differentiated Instruction

▶ **Approaching** Provide guided questions to students as they brainstorm ideas for the skits. Allow students additional time to rehearse their skits.

▶ **Beyond** Encourage students to lead their groups by making sure they have covered all of the checklist items. Beyond-level students can also write a "script" for the skit so that students will know their lines.

▶ **ELL** If students are not familiar with skits, give a brief description. Work with students individually or in their small group to help them rehearse their lines.

Response to Intervention

BIG IDEA   People's actions affect others.

If . . . students cannot give a substantiated response to the Big Idea, "People's actions affect others."

. . . .

Then . . . write several phrases that describe actions discussed in the unit. Have students sort the actions into two groups: *actions that are helpful* and *actions that could hurt others*. Then have students describe the effects of each action with a small group. Following the discussion, allow students to respond to the Big Idea again.

networks

Go to connected.mcgraw-hill.com for additional resources:

• Games
• Assessment
• Videos
• Group Technology Project

Name _____ Date _____

Citizenship Skit Rubric

4 Exemplary	3 Accomplished	2 Developing	1 Beginning
The skit: ☐ accurately depicts a theme about good citizenship at home, school, or in the community. ☐ is well organized with a strong beginning, middle, and end. ☐ demonstrates a strong sense of group work, rehearsal, and performance.	**The skit:** ☐ closely depicts a theme about good citizenship at home, school, or in the community. ☐ provides a fairly well-organized structure with a beginning, middle, and end. ☐ attempts to demonstrate a strong sense of group work, rehearsal, and performance.	**The skit:** ☐ somewhat depicts a theme about good citizenship at home, school, or in the community. ☐ is somewhat organized with a beginning, middle, and end. ☐ is somewhat lacking of a strong sense of group work, rehearsal, and performance.	**The skit:** ☐ attempts to depict a theme about good citizenship at home, school, or in the community. ☐ is not well-organized and lacks a beginning, middle, or end. ☐ shows a weak sense of group work, rehearsal, and performance.

Grading Comments: _____

_____

_____

_____

_____

_____

_____

_____

_____

_____

Project Score: _____

Teacher Notes

Picture Glossary

A

activity   An activity is something we do for fun.

affect   Affect means to make something happen.

authority   Authority means to have the power to make decisions.

B

barter   Barter means to give something and get something else in return.

142

buyers   Buyers are people who use money to buy goods and services.

C

cardinal directions   Cardinal directions are the directions of north, south, east, and west.

N
W · E
S

celebration   A celebration is a special way to honor a person, place, or event.

character   Character means having or showing honesty, courage, or responsibility.

choice   A choice is something to pick from.

citizen   A citizen is a person who belongs to a country.

143

Picture Glossary

community   A community is a place where people live, work, and play.

compass rose   A compass rose shows the four cardinal directions.

N
W E
S

conflict   A conflict is a problem between two or more people.

*courage   Courage means to do something without fear.

culture   Culture is the way a group of people live. It is made up of a group's special food, music, and art.

144

Picture Glossary

D   ***decision**   A decision is a choice to be made.

democracy   A democracy is a government that is run by its people.

E   ***element**   An element is a part of something.

exaggerate   Exaggerate means to make something bigger or more important than it is.

*exchange   Exchange means to give up something for something else.

F   **fable**   A fable is a made-up story that teaches a lesson.

145

Picture Glossary

*fact   A fact is something that is true and not made up.

fiction   Fiction is something that is not true.

G

globe   A globe is a round model of Earth.

goods   Goods are things people buy or grow to sell.

government   A government is a group of people who run a community, state, or country.

H

history   History is the story of people and events from other times and places.

Picture Glossary

holiday   A holiday is a day when we remember and honor a special event or person. (p. 24)

*honesty   Honesty means to be honest or truthful.

L

law   A law is a rule that everyone must follow.

location   A location is a place on Earth.

M

map   A map is a drawing of a place.

Picture Glossary

map key A map key is a list of shapes and symbols used on a map. A map key is also called a map legend.

*model A model is a small copy of something.

money Money is something we use to buy goods and services.

N

nonfiction Nonfiction tells about something true.

O

opportunity cost Opportunity cost is what people give up to do or have something else.

P

peninsula A peninsula is land with water on all sides except one.

physical environment Physical environment is the land and bodies of water around us.

physical map Physical maps show land and bodies of water.

*pledge A pledge is a promise.

political map Political maps show borders, or lines, between areas.

Picture Glossary

producers Producers are people who make or grow goods to sell.

*provide Provide means to give.

responsibility A responsibility is a duty we have. (pages 38 and 116)

right A right is a freedom we have.

rule A rule tells us what we can and cannot do.

save To save means to keep your money in order to spend it later.

Picture Glossary

scarce When there is not enough of something it is scarce.

season A season is one of the four parts of the year.

seller Sellers are people who sell goods and services.

service A service is work done to help others.

Picture Glossary

slavery   Slavery means that one person takes away another person's freedom.

spend   Spend is to use money to buy something.

symbol   A symbol is something that stands for something else.

T

tall tale   A tall tale is a story that exaggerates details.

technology   Technology is the science of making things faster and easier.

152

Picture Glossary

time line   A time line is a line that shows an order of events.

transportation   Transportation is the way people move from place to place.

W

weather   Weather is how hot, cold, wet, or dry it is outside.

Index

by Dinah Zike

Notebook Foldables®

Strategies for using your Elementary Social Studies Program

- Help students organize information.
- Engage students further with the text.
- Provide an opportunity for enrichment and extension.

How to Construct Notebook Foldables®

Provide students with a copy of the template that corresponds to the activity you wish to teach. Then, direct students to:

1. **Fold** the anchor tab(s) and the information tabs where indicated on the template.
2. **Glue** the anchor tab(s) to the page where indicated.
3. **Cut** the Foldable to separate the information tab(s).

Once students have constructed their Notebook Foldables®, have them complete the activity as described in the Teacher Edition.

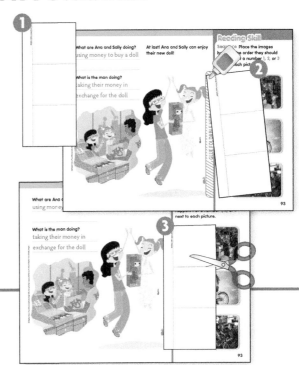

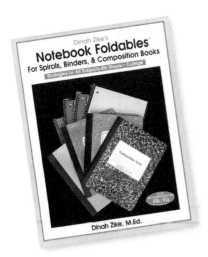

Notebook Foldables® by Dinah Zike

This best-selling book from Dinah Zike features adaptations of her Foldables® specially designed to fit into composition books, spiral notebooks, binders, and even Big Books. The book comes with reproducible graphics and instructions on how to create these modified Foldables® using regular paper. You'll be amazed at the hundreds of full-color examples found throughout the book! This book contains 129 pages complete with templates and a complimentary CD for easy customization and insertion of your own text and graphics.

For more information on this or other Dinah Zike products, visit www.dinah.com or call 1-800-99DINAH.

ISBN-10: 1-882796-27-6

Fold and glue **BEFORE** cutting!

Notebook Foldables® 1A—Use with Unit 1 Lesson 2, page 26.

©2008, DMA; www.dinah.com

Notebook Foldables® 1B—Use with Unit 1 Lesson 4, page 48.

©2008, DMA; www.dinah.com

Fold and glue <u>BEFORE</u> cutting!

Notebook Foldables® 2A—Use with Unit 2 Lesson 1.

©2008, DMA; www.dinah.com

Fold and glue __BEFORE__ cutting!

Notebook Foldables® 2B—Use with Unit 2 Lesson 3.

My Weather

Fold and glue <u>BEFORE</u> cutting!

Notebook Foldables® 3A—Use with Unit 3 Lesson 2.

©2008, DMA; www.dinah.com

Fold and glue <u>BEFORE</u> cutting!

Notebook Foldables® 3B—Use with Unit 3 Lesson 3.

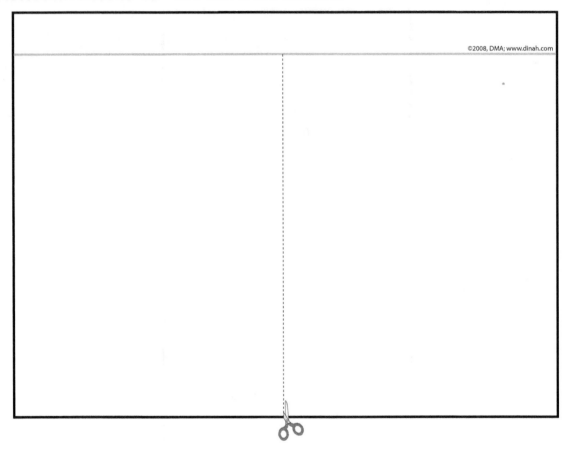

©2008, DMA; www.dinah.com

Fold and glue <u>BEFORE</u> cutting!

Notebook Foldables® 4A—Use with Unit 4 Lesson 1.

©2008, DMA; www.dinah.com

Fold and glue <u>BEFORE</u> cutting!

Notebook Foldables® 4B—Use with Unit 4 Lesson 4.

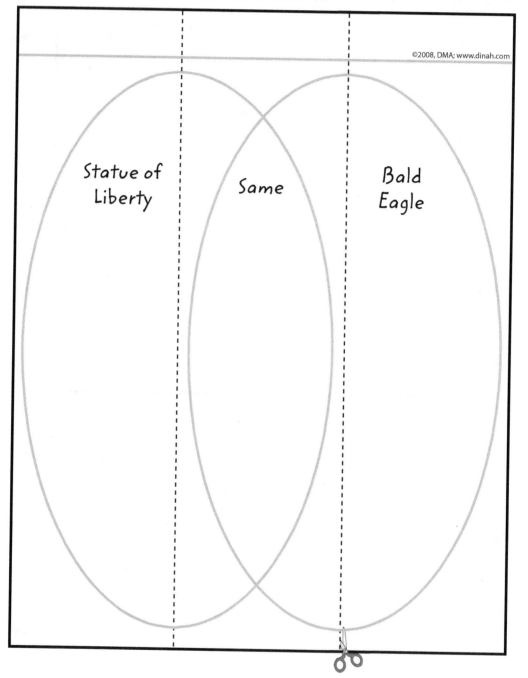

©2008, DMA; www.dinah.com

Statue of Liberty

Same

Bald Eagle

DATE DUE

			PRINTED IN U.S.A.